100 DEADLY SKILLS

The SEAL Operative's Guide
to Eluding Pursuers, Evading Capture,
and Surviving Any Dangerous Situation

Clint Emerson, retired Navy SEAL

Illustrations by Ted Slampyak

TOUCHSTONE

New York London Toronto Sydney New Delhi

Touchstone
An Imprint of Simon & Schuster, Inc.
1230 Avenue of the Americas
New York, NY 10020

First Touchstone trade paperback edition October 2015

TOUCHSTONE and colophon are registered trademarks of Simon & Schuster, Inc.

For information about special discounts for bulk purchases, please contact Simon & Schuster Special Sales at 1-866-506-1949 or business@simonandschuster.com.

The Simon & Schuster Speakers Bureau can bring authors to your live event. For more information or to book an event, contact the Simon & Schuster Speakers Bureau at 1-866-248-3049 or visit our website at www.simonspeakers.com.

Skill testing by Kenzie Emerson
Interior design by Erich Hobbing

Manufactured in the United States of America

10 9 8 7 6 5 4 3 2 1

Library of Congress Cataloging-in-Publication Data
Emerson, Clint.
  100 deadly skills : the SEAL operative's guide / Clint Emerson, retired Navy SEAL ; illustrations by Ted Slampyak.
    pages cm
  Includes bibliographical references and index.
  1. United States. Navy. SEALs—Handbooks, manuals, etc.
2. Survival—Handbooks, manuals, etc. I. Slampyak, Ted, illustrator. II. Title.
III. Title: One hundred deadly skills. IV. Title: SEAL operative's guide.
VG87.E64 2015
613.6'9—dc23
            2015012021

ISBN 978-1-4767-9605-5
ISBN 978-1-4767-9606-2 (ebook)

A Note to Readers

The skills described in the following pages are called "deadly" for a reason—and not just because of the danger they pose to others. Developed by highly trained operatives who regularly face life-threatening conditions, these skills push the limits of human endurance, precision, and ingenuity.

And often, the boundaries of the law.

The book you are holding in your hands (or reading on your device) contains actionable information adapted from the world of special operations. Much of that information, shared here with civilians in the spirit of self-defense, is to be used in only the direst emergencies.

When confronted with unexpected danger, in many cases the safest course of action is escape. In the face of an active shooter (see page 178), the first option (if conditions allow) is to run—and the last is to fight. If a thief wants your valuables, hand them over. If the end of the world truly does come to pass . . . well, then all bets are off.

The author and publisher disclaim any liability from any injury that may result from the use, proper or improper, of the information contained in this book. The stated goal of this book is not to enable a deadly class of citizens but to entertain while simultaneously imparting a body of knowledge that may come in handy in the absolute direst of emergencies.

Be deadly in spirit, but not in action. Respect the rights of others and the laws of the land.

Our fate is determined by how far we are prepared to push ourselves to stay alive—the decisions we make to survive. We must do whatever it takes to endure and make it through alive.

—BEAR GRYLLS

CONTENTS

PART III: INFRASTRUCTURE DEVELOPMENT 47

PART IV: SURVEILLANCE 85

PART V: ACCESS 105

PART VI: COLLECTION 133

PART VII: OPERATIONAL ACTIONS 151

PART VIII: SANITIZATION   189

PART IX: EXFILTRATION AND ESCAPE   209

INTRODUCTION

Potential dangers lurk everywhere these days. Disasters strike in war-torn regions and far-flung locations—but with alarming regularity, they also seem to inch closer and closer to home. Spanning acts of terror, mass shootings, and the unseen (and sometimes virtual) matrix of everyday crime, danger refuses to be confined to dark alleys, unstable nations, or distant zip codes.

People tend to imagine worst-case scenarios in highly colorful terms, but chaos and crime are the real apocalyptic scenarios. We picture aliens, frozen tundra, and intergalactic warfare, when in fact the catastrophic event we've been waiting for is more likely to look like a mundane report of vandalism on last night's news—or the massive Internet shutdown in tomorrow's headlines. Or, indeed, the violent criminal hiding in the shadows of a desolate parking garage. In the face of true catastrophe, a basement full of canned peas and distilled water isn't likely to be much help.

In a future where every stranger poses a potential threat, knowing the predator mindset is the only safe haven. What are the tricks used by the stealthiest, most dangerous human beings in our midst? How can you spot and avoid the dangers that surround us? You could turn to the criminal class to find out. Or you could go one better by taking a page from some of the most highly trained specialists on the planet.

The one hundred deadly skills you are about to encounter are adapted from the world of special operations, a complex web of associations dominated by operatives with a shared predilection for intrigue and danger. These elite, highly skilled warriors are charged with risking their lives under the most challenging and dire conditions on earth. As operatives who routinely infiltrate the world's most dangerous and volatile regions, they must be equal parts spies, soldiers, and lawless rule-breakers.

They are action heroes for modern times, one-part James Bond, the other Rambo. Some call these highly skilled operatives "Violent

Nomads," as a nod to their disregard for international borders and their bias for swift, brutal action.

Many of the techniques that make up the Violent Nomad body of knowledge cannot be divulged without severe risk to public safety, but a great deal of potentially lifesaving information can still be shared. Each skill is broken down into its most critical parts, or Courses of Action (COAs), and summed up by a BLUF (Bottom Line Up Front), which spells out the key takeaway from the operative's perspective; Civilian BLUFs flip the skills around and outline preventive measures civilians can take to arm themselves against predators using these particular techniques.

As a retired Navy SEAL who spent several years inside the NSA (National Security Agency), in writing this book I drew on an unusual breadth of experience that spans twenty years spent running special ops all over the world, both in teams and alone, and merges lessons learned from both combat and surveillance. The skills in this book represent a potential path to survival in the face of any number of dangerous situations, from eluding pursuers and escaping abduction to self-defense. And they may even provide a blueprint for getting through doomsday.

The world isn't getting any safer, but you can be prepared. Whether you're faced with an alien invasion or an assailant wielding a seemingly innocuous item such as a water bottle* or an umbrella, learning how to think like a Violent Nomad will radically improve your chances of coming out on top.

---

* Turn to page 70 if you're interested in developing an irrational fear of water bottles.

PART I

MISSION PREP

001 Anatomy of a Violent Nomad

Beyond the defensive potential common to many of the skills in this book, there is much the average civilian can learn from an operative's mindset. First and foremost, that mindset is defined by preparedness and awareness. Whether in home territory or under deepest cover, operatives are continually scanning the general landscape for threats even when they're not on the clock. Civilians, too, can train their minds toward habits such as scouting exit routes in crowded restaurants or building spur-of-the-moment escape plans. This kind of vigilance allows an operative confronted with sudden danger to take immediate action.

Whether he is crossing borders, executing surveillance, or eliminating dangerous targets and disappearing without a trace, the clandestine operative frequently works alone. Given that he so often finds himself behind enemy lines without reinforcements, an operative's combat and counterintelligence skills are met by an equally sophisticated aptitude for risk assessment and analysis. In an increasingly dangerous world, civilians who are attuned to potential risk (particularly but not exclusively when traveling) will be many steps ahead of the general populace.

The operative also demonstrates a baseline predisposition toward anonymity. Each clandestine operative is trained to "go black," operating for extended periods of time with limited communication to associates. While operating under the radar, he may assume the outward appearance of a student, a businessperson, or a traveler, as he understands that terrorist groups or host-nation governments may be targeting him during his travels—and that if perceived as a spy and arrested, he will be subject to detention and harsh interrogations. Additionally, as a traveler, he is vulnerable to the risks of petty crime and kidnapping that apply to any civilian traveling abroad. To counter such risks, the operative adopts as neutral an appearance as possible. The general rule is the less conspicuous the Nomad, the safer.

No. 001: Anatomy of a Violent Nomad

CONOP (Concept of Operation): Conceal tools of survival and escape in order to decrease exposure to threats.

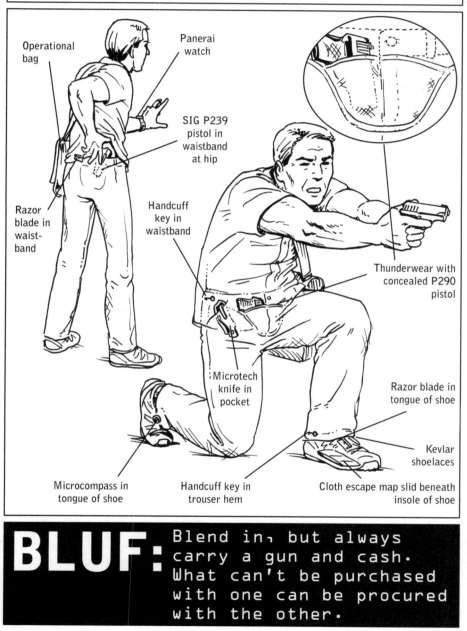

Operational bag

Panerai watch

SIG P239 pistol in waistband at hip

Razor blade in waistband

Handcuff key in waistband

Thunderwear with concealed P290 pistol

Microtech knife in pocket

Razor blade in tongue of shoe

Kevlar shoelaces

Microcompass in tongue of shoe

Handcuff key in trouser hem

Cloth escape map slid beneath insole of shoe

BLUF: Blend in, but always carry a gun and cash. What can't be purchased with one can be procured with the other.

Due to the highly covert nature of their missions, operatives go to great lengths to ensure that they blend into their surroundings. A carefully managed appearance allows them to operate undetected by potential witnesses as well as host-country police and security services. But beyond their unremarkability, clothing and gear must have the capability to conceal the equipment required for an operation or an escape. (The waistband and cuffs of pants and the tongues of shoes, for example, are ideal hiding places for handcuff keys and razor blades.)

Operatives favor brands such as Panerai, which are durable and well made but still have a civilian-friendly look. Always ready to run or fight, they wear closed-toed shoes with Kevlar laces and conceal weapons and spread escape equipment throughout their clothing. Lighters and cigarettes are always carried, even by nonsmokers, as they may be used as a tool of escape or to create a distraction or diversion. (See pages 86, 166, and 168.) LED flashlights are essential for seeing in the dark or signaling for help.

When it comes to gear, preparedness doesn't look quite the way moviegoers have come to expect. Because clandestine operatives cannot board commercial flights with concealed weapons or high-tech spy gear tucked away in their luggage, they favor a "no-tech" or "low-tech" approach that is highly dependent on improvisation. Though fictional spies employ all manner of shiny, complex contraptions, in the real world, every high-tech toy increases an operative's risk of detention or arrest. Hence, operatives learn to adapt, improvise, and overcome technical obstacles using tools and technology that are readily available in the country of operation. One example: Every hotel room has a Bible or a Koran stashed in a bedside drawer—and taping a couple of those together yields a set of improvised body armor that provides significant protection against projectiles.

Though low-tech doesn't usually extend to an operative's communications, he takes a highly cautious approach to cybersecurity. The operative avoids leaving behind trails of digital breadcrumbs at all costs, understanding that any cybercommunication is fundamentally insecure. In an age where savings accounts and the locations of friends and family are vulnerable to any third party with access to a Wi-Fi connection and the will to do harm, there is no such thing as a surfeit of precaution.

Civilian BLUF: Particularly when traveling, civilians are well served by adopting the operative's predilection for anonymity. Choose clothing and accessories for usefulness and general neutrality. In a volatile urban crisis, bright colors and eye-catching logos can become convenient aiming points for a pair of rifle sights.

002 Create an Every Day Carry Kit

While the average civilian approaches emergency preparedness from a life-support perspective that prioritizes food and water supplies (stashed deep in a home basement) to the exclusion of weapons and escape tools, true preparedness acknowledges and confronts the violence of the modern world. To ensure a state of constant preparedness, the Violent Nomad carries up to three types of Every Day Carry (EDC) kits, each designed to support his mission and help him evade crisis. Whether the call comes or not, the EDC kits also provide an edge against unexpected threats of all sorts, from environmental disasters to terrorist strikes and lone-wolf attacks.

When traveling through potentially hostile territory or during turbulent times, a Nomad will distribute several layers of life-support and personal-safety items throughout his clothing and outerwear; in the event that he is stripped of his primary weapon, this practice may leave him with several undetected options of last resort. Escape gear in particular should be spread out in such a way that some of it remains available if the Nomad is restrained.

The most basic kit, the "pocket kit," should be comprised of essential weapons, escape and evasion equipment, and one "black" (covert) mobile phone. Rather than being consolidated into a single container or concealment, these items should be distributed throughout clothing. A handgun should be concealed in a waistband holster, for the most accessible draw. (See page 152 for tips on drawing a holstered weapon.) An emergency communication device is essential, but other contents will vary depending on the terrain. A stainless steel Zebra pen can be used to leave notes for potential rescuers—or to strike an assailant. In the case of abduction or detention, a handcuff key and LED light camouflaged alongside car or hotel keys are potential lifesavers; as backup in the event that clothes pockets are searched, a concealable handcuff key can be hidden in a shirt cuff or on a zipper pull. Some operatives carry mouthpieces, which can be vital during hand-to-hand combat.

The "container kit"—generally tucked into a jacket or an operational bag (see below)—functions as backup in the event that an operative is stripped of his primary weapon and/or operational bag. This highly condensed kit contains small improvised weapons (loose coins tied up in a handkerchief) and navigational aids (a headlamp and a handheld GPS device) that change depending on the environment, as well as lock-picking tools that could provide access to information, food, or shelter. Purchased within the area of operation, a set of "recci" (reconnaissance) key blanks provides an advantage in breaking-and-entering scenarios. Durable and reliably discreet, a rigid sunglass case is the optimal container for this kit.

The final piece of the puzzle is the operational bag. To prepare for the possibility of escape in the face of surveillance or attack, its contents should include an empty collapsible backpack and a change of clothes in colors opposite from the ones the operative is wearing. Even shoes should be taken into consideration—if wearing sneakers, pack a pair of rubber sandals. A concealed pocket holds highly sensitive data on memory devices such as thumb drives or SD cards, a Kevlar clipboard acts as an innocuous-looking form of improvised ballistic armor, and a wad of cash allows the Nomad to subsist in deep cover for as long as the situation demands.

Related Skills: Build a Vehicle Bolt Bag, page 10; Create a Hasty Disguise, page 200; Use Improvised Body Armor, page 20; Identify Emergency Ballistic Shields, page 22.

No. 002: Create an Every Day Carry Kit

CONOP: Acquire and consolidate specific items in order to equip Every Day Carry (EDC) kits.

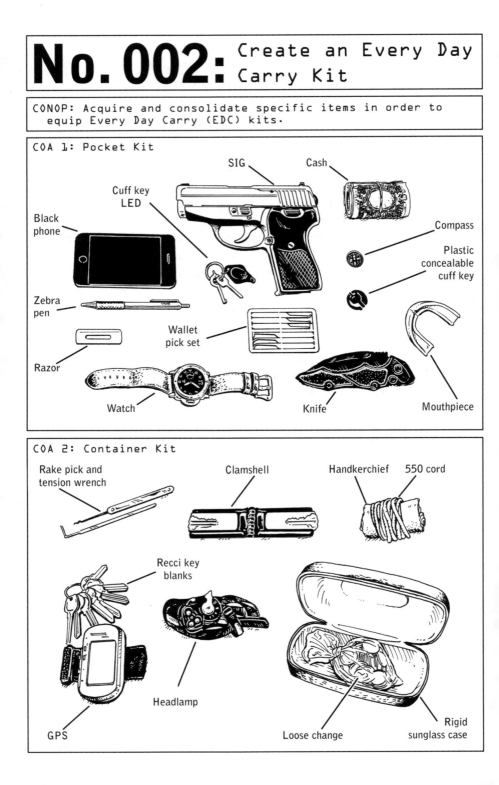

COA 1: Pocket Kit

- SIG
- Cash
- Cuff key LED
- Black phone
- Compass
- Plastic concealable cuff key
- Zebra pen
- Wallet pick set
- Razor
- Watch
- Knife
- Mouthpiece

COA 2: Container Kit

- Rake pick and tension wrench
- Clamshell
- Handkerchief
- 550 cord
- Recci key blanks
- GPS
- Headlamp
- Loose change
- Rigid sunglass case

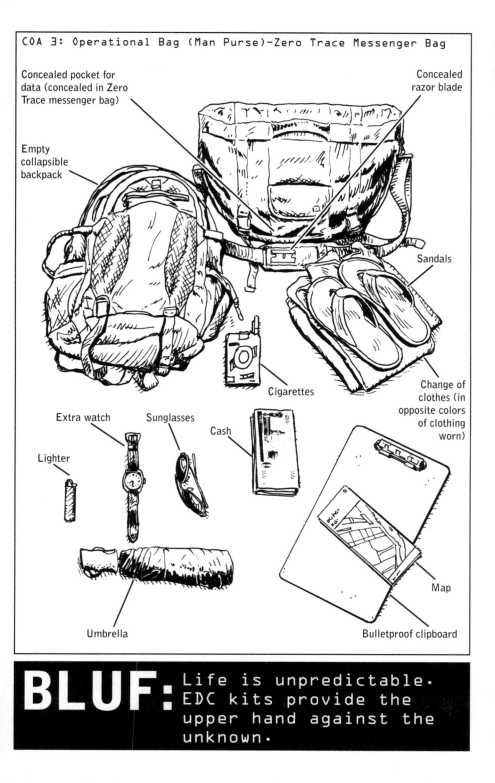

COA 3: Operational Bag (Man Purse)—Zero Trace Messenger Bag

Concealed pocket for data (concealed in Zero Trace messenger bag)

Concealed razor blade

Empty collapsible backpack

Sandals

Cigarettes

Change of clothes (in opposite colors of clothing worn)

Extra watch

Sunglasses

Cash

Lighter

Umbrella

Map

Bulletproof clipboard

BLUF: Life is unpredictable. EDC kits provide the upper hand against the unknown.

003 Build a Vehicle Bolt Bag

Operatives don't have the luxury of being able to return to base to stock up on food or ammunition, so their effectiveness as free-range agents is built around preparation—and preparation means always being prepared for the worst. When an operative is conducting a mission abroad, one of the first orders of business upon being called into action is building a bolt bag. In the case of emergency, this bag (also known as a "bug-out kit") becomes an essential life-support system. It contains everything needed to keep the operative alive, should he have to "go black," hiding out of sight until he can either resume his mission or make arrangements to safely exit the area of operation.

A bolt bag typically consists of a day or two of life support—water, food, cash, emergency medical supplies, navigation aids, and a "black" or covert phone similar to the type known in the criminal world as a "burner." The bag should be stashed in the operational vehicle, concealed in a spot that is easily accessible from the driver's seat, such as the center console compartment (between the seats) or under the seat. (Should the operative find himself upside down as the result of a collision with aggressors, the kit should be within arm's reach.) As its name implies, the bolt bag needs to be light enough to be carried—canned foods and other heavy supplies do not lend themselves to ease of transport.

Civilian BLUF: In day-to-day life, bolt bags can be used as precautionary disaster measures—not only by civilians living in regions at high risk for natural disasters, but by anyone alert to the threat of urban disasters or terrorism.

No. 003: Build a Vehicle Bolt Bag

CONOP: Be ready to move when crisis strikes.

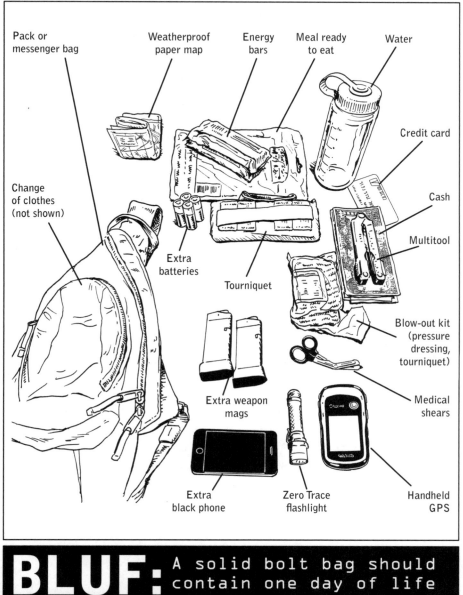

Pack or messenger bag

Weatherproof paper map

Energy bars

Meal ready to eat

Water

Credit card

Cash

Multitool

Change of clothes (not shown)

Extra batteries

Tourniquet

Blow-out kit (pressure dressing, tourniquet)

Medical shears

Extra weapon mags

Extra black phone

Zero Trace flashlight

Handheld GPS

BLUF: A solid bolt bag should contain one day of life support.

004 Make a Concealable Compass

Covert situations often call for easily concealable, dependable low-fi alternatives—and in the case of a compass, a simple pair of magnets fits the bill. An operative may have been stripped of his GPS device upon capture or may be working in a context in which the use of a handheld GPS system would attract too much notice. A concealable compass ensures that the Nomad is always able to effectively navigate through unknown territory, no matter how remote.

Though microcompasses may be found at any adventure store in the developed world, they may not be available elsewhere. Improvised compasses, on the other hand, are easy to make using resources readily available in most countries. The tool works by harnessing the power of rare-earth magnets, the baseline mechanism used to power compasses. Tuned to the dial of the earth's magnetic field, when connected and allowed to dangle from a length of thread, the rods become a natural compass; one points south, the other north.

Because the purchase of rare-earth magnets can arouse suspicion, it is advisable to seek out less alerting products such as refrigerator magnets, whiteboard magnets, or magnetic handbag closures, always in pairs. Any improvisations must be tested thoroughly, lest the Nomad be confronted with an inaccurate improvised tool mid-escape.

Civilian BLUF: The standard instructions for building a compass (see illustration) involve a pair of rare-earth rod magnets and a length of Kevlar thread (chosen for its durability), but a similar effect may be achieved by piercing a magnetized needle through a cork and floating the device in water.

No. 004: Make a Concealable Compass

CONOP: Construct and conceal a fail-safe backup compass.

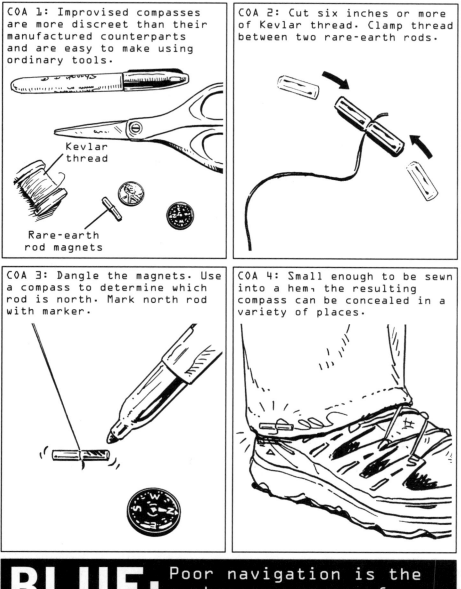

COA 1: Improvised compasses are more discreet than their manufactured counterparts and are easy to make using ordinary tools.

Kevlar thread

Rare-earth rod magnets

COA 2: Cut six inches or more of Kevlar thread. Clamp thread between two rare-earth rods.

COA 3: Dangle the magnets. Use a compass to determine which rod is north. Mark north rod with marker.

COA 4: Small enough to be sewn into a hem, the resulting compass can be concealed in a variety of places.

BLUF: Poor navigation is the number-one cause of recapture after escape.

005 Build an Improvised Concealable Holster

Operatives are well versed in using underground channels to acquire weapons within the area of operation, as guns and other munitions cannot be transported across international borders without permission from both the country of origin and the destination country. But specialized equipment such as concealable holsters are often harder to come by, and any attempt to smuggle them in would certainly get a Nomad pulled into an unwanted detainment at customs.

In order to maintain a low profile, operatives generally travel as lightly as possible, utilizing off-the-shelf resources to fulfill their mission requirements. This predisposition toward minimalism presents challenges but does not tend to leave operatives in a disadvantaged position, as many improvised tools—the holster included—provide a better capability than manufactured versions.

Commercially available holsters tend to make concealment difficult. Bulky and inflexible, they increase the overall signature of the weapon in an operative's waistline and can make extraction a challenge. A pistol that cannot be quickly and seamlessly removed from an operative's holster becomes a deadly liability, so the choice of holster is crucial. This improvised model, made of wire hanger and tape, contributes virtually no additional bulk and ensures a quick and glitch-free draw.

Related Skills: Draw a Concealed Pistol, page 152.

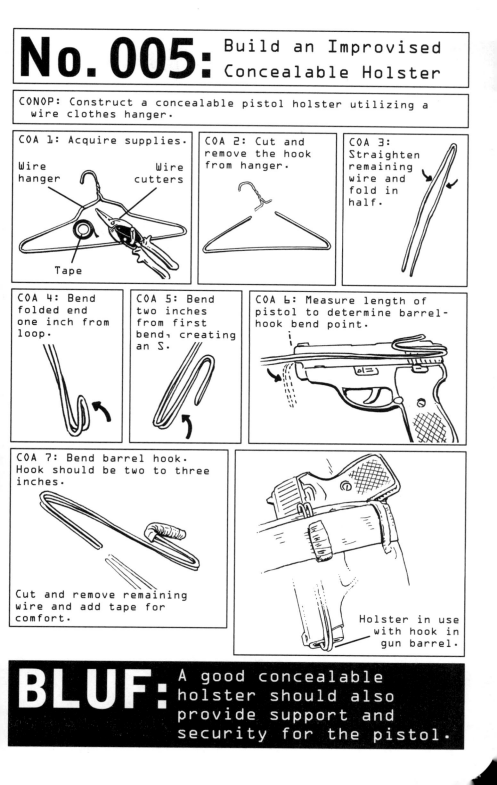

No. 005: Build an Improvised Concealable Holster

CONOP: Construct a concealable pistol holster utilizing a wire clothes hanger.

COA 1: Acquire supplies.

Wire hanger
Wire cutters
Tape

COA 2: Cut and remove the hook from hanger.

COA 3: Straighten remaining wire and fold in half.

COA 4: Bend folded end one inch from loop.

COA 5: Bend two inches from first bend, creating an S.

COA 6: Measure length of pistol to determine barrel-hook bend point.

COA 7: Bend barrel hook. Hook should be two to three inches.

Cut and remove remaining wire and add tape for comfort.

Holster in use with hook in gun barrel.

BLUF: A good concealable holster should also provide support and security for the pistol.

The possibility of being captured, kidnapped, or taken hostage exists for all travelers, but it's one that's especially real for operatives who cannot rely upon being bailed out by their home-nation governments.

If captured, operatives can expect to be immediately frisked for concealed weapons, at which point they are likely to have most of their gear confiscated by their captors. Escape aids concealed in clothing may remain undetected for a while, but operatives know that if they are in captivity long enough, they will eventually be stripped naked and have to rely solely upon the escape tools they've concealed on and inside their bodies. Given a lack of institutional backup, self-escape preparations are an essential component of a Nomad's every operational plan.

A human aversion to bloody bandages means captors are unlikely to closely examine lesions or scars, so a Nomad can utilize medical adhesive to glue specific tools onto the body underneath manufactured wounds.

There is also a near-universal reluctance on the part of captors for frisking, patting down, or probing the nether regions of their detainees—and this unease provides operatives with exploitable opportunities for concealment of escape tools in axilla (armpit) hair or pubic hair. Body concealments can be as elaborate as suppositories placed in the penis (urethra and foreskin), vagina, or rectum or in the nostrils, ears, mouth, and navel. And they can be as simple as barely perceptible condoms. Note: This advantage can work to a Nomad's benefit, but diminishes quickly as he or she is transferred to increasingly higher levels of detention and security.

Related Skills: Construct a Rectal Concealment, page 18.

No. 006: Conceal Escape Tools

CONOP: Conceal escape tools on and within the body.

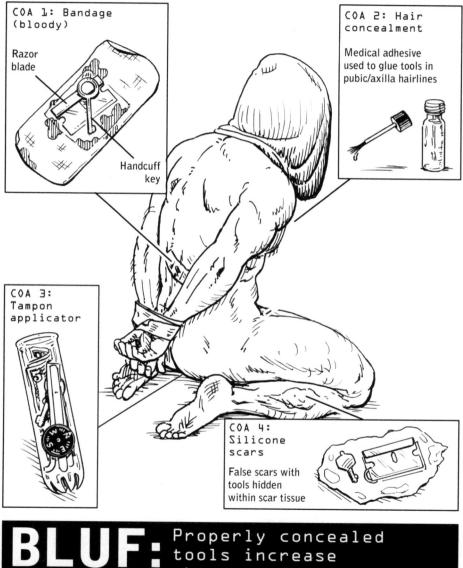

COA 1: Bandage (bloody)

Razor blade

Handcuff key

COA 2: Hair concealment

Medical adhesive used to glue tools in pubic/axilla hairlines

COA 3: Tampon applicator

COA 4: Silicone scars

False scars with tools hidden within scar tissue

BLUF: Properly concealed tools increase chances of a successful escape.

007 Construct a Rectal Concealment

When a mission involves a high potential for capture, operatives prepare for the possibility that they will be detained, searched, and stripped of any visible weapons. This leaves the operative only one method of recourse: the concealment of weapons and escape tools in his bodily cavities. Navigation aids, money, escape tools, and even makeshift weapons such as an improvised ice pick (see illustration) can be concealed inside a tampon applicator or aluminum cigar tube that is inserted into the anal cavity.

The use of the rectal passage as a hiding place for illegal items or weapons is common in the shadow worlds of drug trafficking and terrorism. But the technique is also well known to operatives as an extreme measure of self-preservation used during ground zero of high-risk missions.

Such a concealment is surprisingly immune to high-tech methods of detection. Full-body scanners bounce electromagnetic waves off the body in search of metallic objects and other contraband. While their low-frequency radar can detect weapons that protrude from the body, it cannot see through skin or bone. Even X-ray machines don't do a very good job of rendering items camouflaged in tissue, and MRI machines used in medical contexts would render a concealment as a shadow that, given its location, could be mistaken for fecal matter.

Note: Any improvised containers must be waterproof, nontoxic, smooth, and sealed on their upper end.

No. 007: Construct a Rectal Concealment

CONOP: Conceal lifesaving tools in body cavities.

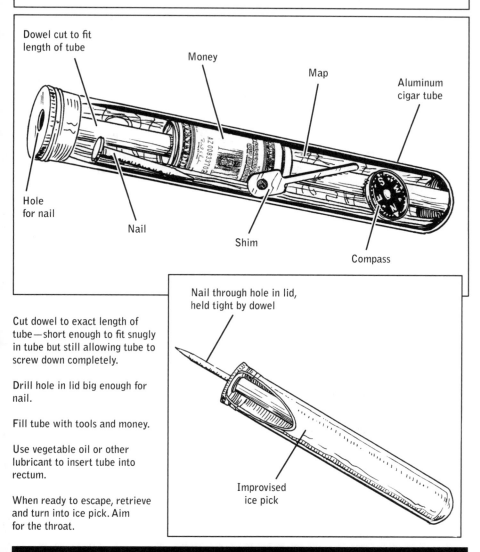

Dowel cut to fit length of tube

Money

Map

Aluminum cigar tube

Hole for nail

Nail

Shim

Compass

Nail through hole in lid, held tight by dowel

Cut dowel to exact length of tube—short enough to fit snugly in tube but still allowing tube to screw down completely.

Drill hole in lid big enough for nail.

Fill tube with tools and money.

Use vegetable oil or other lubricant to insert tube into rectum.

When ready to escape, retrieve and turn into ice pick. Aim for the throat.

Improvised ice pick

BLUF: Exploit the fact that captors may be squeamish about searching body cavities.

008 Use Improvised Body Armor

Whether engaging armed targets or caught in the crossfire of social unrest, operatives frequently find themselves in need of body armor. Government-issued armor provides the best protection against injury—but because of its traceability, operatives on covert missions are not authorized to use it. To survive, they must learn to create improvised body armor using everyday items and materials.

When taped tightly together in units of two, hardcover books such as encyclopedias and dictionaries become rigid bundles or "plates" that can dissipate the energy of a projectile. Taping commonly available ceramic tiles to the outer facing of each plate provides an additional layer of protection, and the resulting armor can be concealed by a jacket or coat or easily carried in a messenger bag or backpack.

Plates should be suspended on the front and back of the torso in order to protect "center mass"—the spine and vital organs such as heart and lungs.

Another layer of protection can be achieved via a commercially available Kevlar clipboard rated to stop 9mm pistol bullets. Lightweight and portable, once painted with a flat brown paint the clipboard is non-alerting and will pass scrutiny if examined at a border crossing or airport.

Improvised armor must be thick enough to slow or stop a projectile and thin enough to be wearable. Depending on available materials, Violent Nomads may be able to create improvised armor thick enough to stop a projectile. Pistol rounds travel more slowly (9mm projectile at 1,100 feet per second); faster rifle rounds (5.56mm projectile at approximately 3,000 feet per second) require more protective material. But an operative never quite knows what he will encounter, and so tends to build for the worst-case scenario.

No. 008: Use Improvised Body Armor

CONOP: Build expedient body armor using everyday items.

COA 1: Acquire hardback books, duct tape, and ceramic tiles.

COA 2: Tape two or more books together to create one plate. Construct two plates. Tape on a layer of ceramic tiles.

Ceramic tiles

COA 3: Add shoulder straps made of tape to create a body-armor system.

Secure system to body by wrapping horizontal layers of duct tape.

Tape a double layer of tape to itself to prevent the straps from sticking to your shoulders.

COA 4: Conduct jump test and add tape as needed to increase integrity.

BLUF: As a method of last resort, operatives can use hardcover books to deflect projectiles.

009 Identify Emergency Ballistic Shields

When bullets are flying, the odds of survival are determined by split-second decisions. Whether those decisions are educated ones, rather than unconscious moves made in the clutches of fight or flight, can mean the difference between safety and serious injury or death.

The instinct to run for cover is universal, but it must be coupled with an understanding of the relationship between ballistics and everyday materials. Dense wood, concrete, steel, and granite are the preferred materials in the face of open fire—these thick, heavy materials can stop bullets and save lives. Sheetrock walls may offer concealment—thus diminishing a shooter's accuracy—and give the appearance of solidity, but they will not stop bullets. Even a small .22-caliber pistol can rip through drywall. Concrete or steel columns, on the other hand, provide better ballistic protection, despite their relative lack of coverage.

In cases of emergency, these principles can be applied to many of the objects in civilian environments. Granite-top tables, concrete planters, and steel appliances all fit the bill. Countertops, desks, and tables in hotel rooms are frequently made of granite or steel. But some everyday objects appear solid yet are made out of lightweight materials that won't hold up to gunfire. Mailboxes and trash cans are generally made out of aluminum. Hulking vending machines are mostly comprised of glass and plastic. Cars are partially made of steel, but a steel so lightweight that it fails to offer adequate protection; in the absence of other options, hiding behind the engine side of the car, rather than the empty trunk, puts an additional layer of dense materials between an operative or civilian and the shooter.

Related Skills: Use Improvised Body Armor, page 20; Survive an Active Shooter, page 178.

No. 009: Identify Emergency Ballistic Shields

CONOP: Know where to take cover when caught in crossfire.

COA 1: Bullet-slowing and -stopping materials

Dense wood
Concrete
Steel
Granite

COA 2: Know the difference between cover and concealment. Cover stops bullets, concealment doesn't.

Concrete and steel: cover
Drywall: concealment

COA 3: Identify and use makeshift structures while at home or in public.

Granite-top table
NOT sofa

Engine-side of car
NOT trunk-side

Concrete planter
NOT trash can

COA 4: Acquire bulletproof materials and disguise as everyday items.

Backed with bulletproof plates

Mica clipboard

Hardcover book

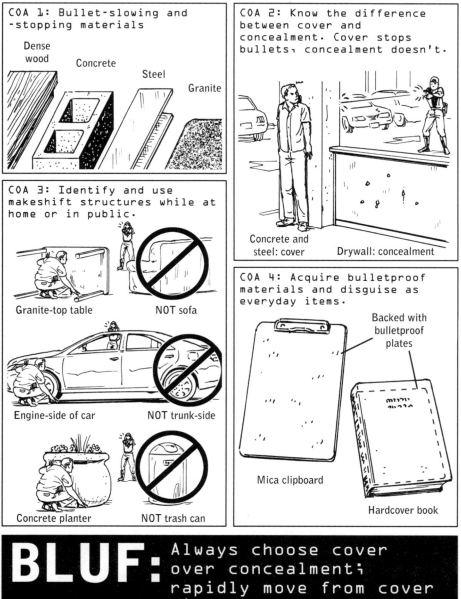

BLUF: Always choose cover over concealment; rapidly move from cover to cover.

010 The Violent Nomad Workout

No strangers to ruthless obstacle courses and drills that combine sleep deprivation and live explosives to simulate the hardships of real-world combat, operatives are trained under the toughest conditions on earth. Once past basic training, they remain combat-ready by incorporating the "Run Fight Run" formula into their workouts.

Repeatedly lifting a pair of dumbbells doesn't translate into an ability to defeat an assailant in hand-to-hand combat after an arduous chase over rugged terrain—so Violent Nomad training prizes real-world combat and self-defense techniques over muscle-building reps. Traditional strength-building and cardiovascular exercises have their place, but integrating the Run Fight Run philosophy into workout routines builds the endurance to outlast an opponent in a fight and/or chase.

Consisting of integrated repetitive striking movements stacked with sprints, Run Fight Run workouts do not require a gym or any sophisticated equipment. All that's needed is a place to sprint and an object to carry and strike, preferably a heavy punching bag; designed for striking, it is versatile enough to be used for squats, dead lifts, carrying, and presses. A heavy bag can also be thrown and struck on the ground, which is where most fights end up.

Civilian BLUF: Use the heavy bag to perform a mix of exercises, with sprints integrated between reps. Increase duration and weight as needed to ramp up intensity over time. A worthy conditioning goal is to be able to perform three sets of striking for three minutes straight and then sprint for one mile in seven minutes or less.

No. 010: The Violent Nomad Workout

CONOP: Use a stacked workout to simulate fighting conditions.

Hanging heavy bag strikes, one minute

Sprint half mile

Grounded heavy bag strikes, one minute

Sprint half mile

Heavy bag bear hug carry, one minute

Sprint half mile

BLUF: A "Run Fight Run" philosophy builds endurance for hand-to-hand combat.

PART II

INFILTRATION: ACCESS TO ENEMY TERRITORY

011 Cross Enemy Borders by Sea

As smugglers and refugees the world over well know, maritime borders in even the most secure countries tend to display high degrees of porosity. For an operative bent on discretion and stealth, in the right kind of landscape helo casting becomes a preferential method of entry.

Dropping from a slow-moving helicopter into frigid waters is a high-level, dangerous skill. Even while hovering, helicopters can create hurricanelike winds that result in blinding mists and skin-stinging water blasts. Practice is essential, and leaping out of a helicopter into dark seas requires proper altitude and safe forward speed. Only by following specific protocols can operatives survive the jump. At an altitude of twenty feet, the helicopter's forward speed should not exceed ten knots; at an altitude of ten feet, forward speed should not exceed twenty knots. This is known as the "10 for 20, 20 for 10" rule.

Correct body positioning (see diagram) prevents injury and ensures that the force of impact hits the diving fins (rather than any protruding body parts) and does not dislodge the diving mask. Although the jump prohibits the use of heavy-duty diving equipment, a wetsuit, a mask or goggles, fins, and an inflatable life jacket are essential. All other gear must be stowed in a waterproof backpack or "dry bag" and strapped onto the operative with lanyards so as to prevent its being lost to the depth of the ocean. Its contents should include mission-specific gear such as a change of clothes that will allow the operative to blend into the area of operation and an additional weapon, along with a hand shovel. The operative's primary weapon, an MP7 submachine gun, should be loaded and carried bolt forward; a condom stretched over its muzzle prevents water from entering the barrel but won't impede a bullet's exit path.

The dry bag is slung over one shoulder so it can easily be shed if the operative runs into difficulties in the water. Strapping a bag on too securely could impede the operative's swimming stroke and pose a risk of drowning.

To swim to shore, operatives use the combat recovery stroke, a side stroke with a minimized profile in which the arms don't exit the water. Once out of the water, they change into dry clothes and use the hand shovel to cache their gear.

No. 011: Cross Enemy Borders by Sea

CONOP: Conduct aquatic border crossing without detection.

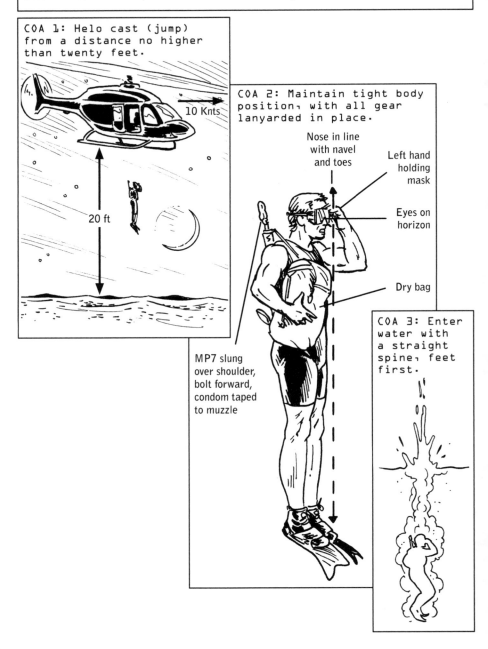

COA 1: Helo cast (jump) from a distance no higher than twenty feet.

10 Knts

20 ft

COA 2: Maintain tight body position, with all gear lanyarded in place.

Nose in line with navel and toes

Left hand holding mask

Eyes on horizon

Dry bag

MP7 slung over shoulder, bolt forward, condom taped to muzzle

COA 3: Enter water with a straight spine, feet first.

COA 4: Swim to shore utilizing combat recovery stroke.

Change of clothes

Shoes

GPS

Hand shovel

Pistol

Extra weapon magazines

Black phone

COA 5: Change out of clothes and cache swim gear. Dress to blend into environment.

Swim gear buried (cached)

BLUF: Unprotected beaches provide easy entry into areas of interest.

012 Cross Enemy Borders by Air

For most civilians, illegal border crossings conjure up tunnels dug deep underground, passage fees paid to shadowy guides, and caravan rides to distant way stations. But for Violent Nomads, border crossings are solitary affairs best accomplished via a territory's most unmonitored, unguarded spaces: by sea (page 28), by land (page 34), or by air. When executed in a country's desolate corners and under cover of darkness, such infiltrations can be entirely undetectable.

For trained operatives, an infiltration by air is built on a two-pronged approach: appropriation of an unmanned private plane (page 66) and descent via wingsuit and parachute.

Global laws dictate that maritime airspace reverts to international rule within twelve nautical miles of any country's coastline—and that guideline should inform any attempt at infiltration. Once within enemy airspace, the aircraft must "go black," its transponder, radios, and lights shut off in order to avoid alerting enemy air-traffic control towers to its presence.

A combination of airgliding and parachuting from the plane down onto rural terrain offers the quietest and least visible means of entry. Once a landing point has been identified, calculating the jump point involves a universal equation: When jumping from a moving aircraft in a wingsuit made out of a nonporous nylon, every two and a half feet dropped means a simultaneous gain of one foot of forward glide, more if going downwind. Such a suit essentially turns an operative into a human kite, allowing him to use his legs and arms to steer like an aircraft. Parachuting is a slow-moving and much more visible proposition, so a Nomad should wait until the last possible minute to activate his chute.

Once on ground, the nylon wingsuit and parachute can be melted into a handful of glasslike beads.

No. 012: Cross Enemy Borders by Air

CONOP: Infiltrate territory via unmonitored airspace.

COA 1: Using the world's most common aircraft—the Cessna 152—fly within twelve miles of target country or area at ten thousand feet.

COA 2: Turn all radios, lights, and transponder to off position.

COA 3: Level and trim aircraft on a heading out to sea or into rural terrain. Exit aircraft and fly suit toward rural border.

COA 4: Open chute and land inside enemy territory.

COA 5: Melt and bury wing-suit and parachute. Blend in.

BLUF: Airspace provides numerous unmonitored points of access into many countries.

013 Cross Enemy Borders by Land

Every nation displays some weaknesses along its borders, particularly in its uninhabited spaces, and operatives always seek to exploit these vulnerabilities. But the wilder the terrain, the more challenging it will be to cross. A seasoned operative crossing enemy borders on foot might spend days or weeks trekking alone through scorching deserts, freezing mountaintops, and dense jungle as he slowly wends his way toward the area of operation. Despite the pace and physical challenges of such an approach, the most difficult route is likely to be the most desirable one—for the more rugged the terrain, the freer it will be from scrutiny and surveillance. If airspace is heavily guarded, infiltration on land may also be the operative's only recourse.

Gear and Transportation: Almost inevitably, a portion of the journey will occur on foot, but the ideal scenario will allow the operative to clock a fair number of miles on an off-road motorbike with the horsepower to carry a two- to three-hundred-pound load and the durability to take on extremely uneven terrain. In many parts of the world, motorcycles are more common than cars, so acquiring or stealing a bike from a neighboring country is well within the operative's grasp.

In addition to his EDC kit and bolt bag (pages 6 and 10), the operative will be carrying enough fuel, food, and water to last the trip and the clothing and gear needed in order to disguise himself once he crosses the border; even if the operative is able to forgo drinking water because water sources are common throughout the terrain, his mission supplies will be extensive. Each phase of the infiltration will also require a unique set of tools and weather-appropriate gear.

No. 013: Cross Enemy Borders by Land

CONOP: Penetrate landlocked borders via difficult terrain.

COA 1: Cross-country motorcycles provide the ability to carry fuel and gear over challenging terrain.

COA 2: Multiday crossings will require night movement and daylight rest. Improvised shelters become paramount.

Snow blocks cut from trench

Insulating material

Snow Trench Shelter

COA 3: Track progress by pace counting if GPS fails.

COA 4: Walk on dry ground or transit during rain or snowstorms to ensure no consistent footprints are left behind.

BLUF: The more difficult the terrain, the better the odds of discreet infiltration.

Shelter: Though operatives are trained to survive extreme levels of sleep deprivation, an infiltration stretching over several days or longer necessitates rest stops.

Improvised shelters are usually preferred. Unlike nylon tents, shelters built from found materials such as branches or compacted snow blend into their environments and act as camouflage. In snow-covered landscapes, igloo-like shelters can be constructed out of compacted blocks of snow. Despite their temperature, these blocks act as nonporous shields that effectively shut out exterior weather while sealing in heat, allowing operatives to warm the shelter with their own body heat and the addition of a lit candle or two. Once the slabs of snow are placed back into the snow bank, exposure to a few hours of sun, rain, or snow takes care of covering the operative's tracks.

Navigation: When the terrain dictates that operatives proceed on foot, the most grueling portion of the multiphase infiltration process has begun. Operatives may walk for days in extreme weather conditions to reach their destination. (In fact, poor weather conditions may be optimal as a means of erasing the operative's footprints.) And they must be prepared to navigate using only a compass and a map in the event that their GPS device fails.

This proves much easier in mountainous areas or seascapes, where mountaintops and other topographical landmarks provide reference points for orientation. In undifferentiated desert environments that stretch out for hundreds of miles, the risk of straying far off course or even walking in circles is significant.

In such instances, pace counting—the practice of counting every other step as a gauge of distance—can be a lifesaving technique. A single adult step spans approximately one meter, so one hundred double-steps add up to approximately two hundred meters. Keeping track can be an effective barometer of distance in an environment with few other means of assessing progress.

Untraceability: Operatives generally travel under cover of night, sleeping for short stretches during daylight hours and timing their night movements to lunar cycles when they can. A half-moon offers a level of visibility that is particularly welcome on rough terrain, while full moons may render the operative too visible. Night travel is significantly slower than daytime movements but involves fewer risks than traveling in broad daylight.

Operatives also plan their routes through terrain that makes detection difficult and take precautions to avoid leaving clues behind. They urinate off-route, in bodies of water if possible, and pack and carry their fecal matter. Where terrain permits, they avoid soil, sand, and mud and walk on nonprinting surfaces such as rocks, roots, grass, leaves, and bark. Footprints are unavoidable, but operatives try to break up a consistent trail anytime the environment permits.

014 Conceal Gear Using Caches

A Violent Nomad's mission is complete only once he has successfully vanished from the area of operation—so he never undertakes an infiltration without a well-planned exit strategy that accounts for all of his post-mission needs. Traveling light is crucial, so particularly when crossing into remote territory on foot, the Nomad will separate his gear and supplies into two categories: items needed for the first leg of his journey, and items needed post-mission and/or for emergency exfiltration. Designed to support survival on the run, his secondary cache will store a well-thought-out resupply of food, fuel, communication devices, money, and weapons, hidden away on a preplanned route out of town.

Operational gear reserved for future use can be cached via a variety of methods. Protected from the elements by being packed into durable containers such as water bottles or lengths of PVC pipe, it can be concealed anywhere from caves to hollowed-out tree trunks to the bottoms of lakes. The more remote the cache site the better, as the last thing a Nomad wants to do is recover a cache that has been booby-trapped or put under surveillance. Burying operational gear well out of sight reduces the odds of accidental discovery. Marking its location on a GPS device enables the Nomad to recover his gear in the absence of visible landmarks.

No. 014: Conceal Gear Using Caches

CONOP: Properly cache operational gear or future life-support items.

COA 1: Construction

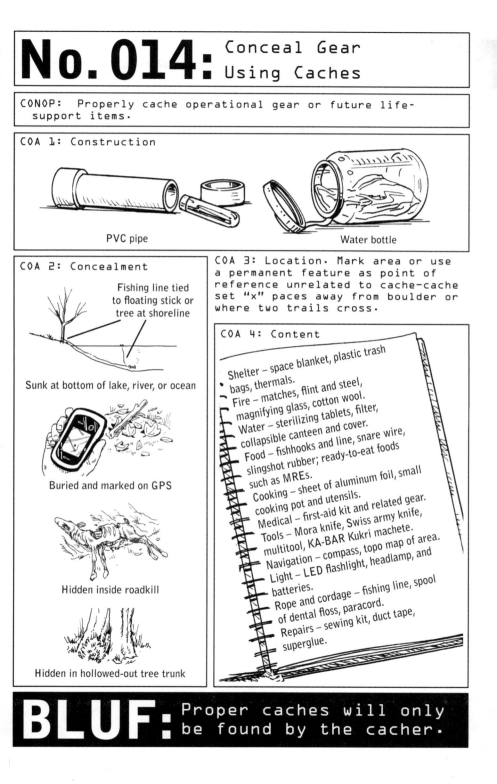

PVC pipe

Water bottle

COA 2: Concealment

Fishing line tied to floating stick or tree at shoreline

Sunk at bottom of lake, river, or ocean

Buried and marked on GPS

Hidden inside roadkill

Hidden in hollowed-out tree trunk

COA 3: Location. Mark area or use a permanent feature as point of reference unrelated to cache-cache set "x" paces away from boulder or where two trails cross.

COA 4: Content

Shelter – space blanket, plastic trash bags, thermals.
Fire – matches, flint and steel, magnifying glass, cotton wool.
Water – sterilizing tablets, filter, collapsible canteen and cover.
Food – fishhooks and line, snare wire, slingshot rubber; ready-to-eat foods such as MREs.
Cooking – sheet of aluminum foil, small cooking pot and utensils.
Medical – first-aid kit and related gear.
Tools – Mora knife, Swiss army knife, multitool, KA-BAR Kukri machete.
Navigation – compass, topo map of area.
Light – LED flashlight, headlamp, and batteries.
Rope and cordage – fishing line, spool of dental floss, paracord.
Repairs – sewing kit, duct tape, superglue.

BLUF: Proper caches will only be found by the cacher.

015 Hook and Climb a Target Structure

Nomads frequently gain access to multi-occupancy target buildings by strolling into unlocked lobbies or picking rudimentary commercial locks (see page 110) on back doors. But in highly secured buildings monitored by camera and/or roving patrol, access through front or back doors may not be negotiable.

Fortunately, any building with a row of balconies along its back side presents a secondary option: scaling the exterior of the building from balcony to balcony. Using a painter's pole, an extra-long length of tubular nylon or rope, and a hook, a Nomad can construct a lightweight ladder system that will safely hold his body weight—enabling him to perform the simple "hook and climb" technique used for centuries by pirates stealing onto enemy ships.

Tying a series of frost knots into a doubled-over length of tubular nylon (its bitter ends tied together with an overhand knot) yields a durable stepladder (see diagram); the line should be more than twice the length of the target structure's height. After a heavyweight metal household hook is inserted into a painter's pole and tied or snapped onto the ladder, the apparatus can be hooked onto an upper structure durable enough to hold the operative's weight. He then climbs from one floor to the next and repeats the process until the target destination is reached.

Even when performed late at night, this method of last resort comes with a high possibility of exposure. But because security cameras typically aren't set up to catch people climbing into a building, in a high-security context it may still be the best option for a Nomad looking to act with stealth. Building owners seldom set up cameras beyond the first floor—and train those they do install toward doorways, on the assumption that any invaders will be coming in through the ground floor.

No. 015: Hook and Climb a Target Structure

CONOP: Improvise an ascent device for a multilevel structure.

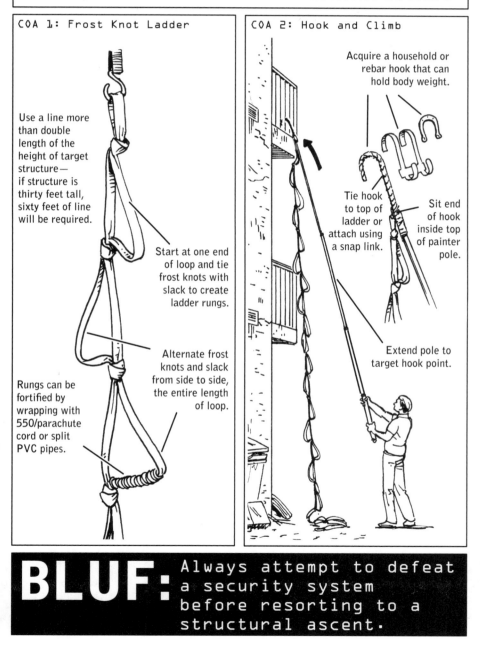

COA 1: Frost Knot Ladder

Use a line more than double length of the height of target structure—if structure is thirty feet tall, sixty feet of line will be required.

Start at one end of loop and tie frost knots with slack to create ladder rungs.

Alternate frost knots and slack from side to side, the entire length of loop.

Rungs can be fortified by wrapping with 550/parachute cord or split PVC pipes.

COA 2: Hook and Climb

Acquire a household or rebar hook that can hold body weight.

Tie hook to top of ladder or attach using a snap link.

Sit end of hook inside top of painter pole.

Extend pole to target hook point.

BLUF: Always attempt to defeat a security system before resorting to a structural ascent.

While a smooth building facade or high wall may not offer an operative the convenience of climbing from balcony to balcony (see page 40), the use of a one-way friction knot makes infiltration via rope or drainpipe eminently feasible—so long as the climbing rope is taut and securely anchored at both top and bottom ends.

A safety knot used by rock climbers as a form of lifesaving backup, the Prusik knot is tied in such a way that it can move only up a rope or line; downward pressure causes it to lock into place. Tied to a climber's harness, the knot can provide a fail-safe that may catch the climber in the event that other devices fail. In an infiltration or escape scenario, the knot can be exploited for its ability to slide up a line, locking into place when it receives the operative's body weight.

To tie a Prusik knot, first tie a shoelace or an equivalent length of small-gauge nylon or parachute cord into a loop using a square knot (see page 43). Then, wrap the cord around the climbing rope or drainpipe and loop the cord through itself (see diagram). Pass the cord through the resulting loop twice more. Pull tightly.

Ideally, tie four Prusik knots to use as hand- and footholds, as when shimmying up the line. In the event that supplies are limited (if using shoelaces in the case of escape), two knots are enough to toggle from a single handhold to a single foothold.

If shimmying up a drainpipe, it will be necessary to untie and retie knots around support brackets. To save time, bring extra pre-looped cord.

No. 016: Scale a High Wall

CONOP: Ascend multilevel structures using improvised devices.

COA 1: Tie four Prusik knots: two for hands, two for feet. The one-way friction knot will slide up but not down.

COA 2: Slide hands up to eye level, pull knees to chest, and stand up in loops. Slide hands up to eye level and repeat.

COA 3: Prusik knots can work on drainpipes, too, but must be untied and retied around support brackets.

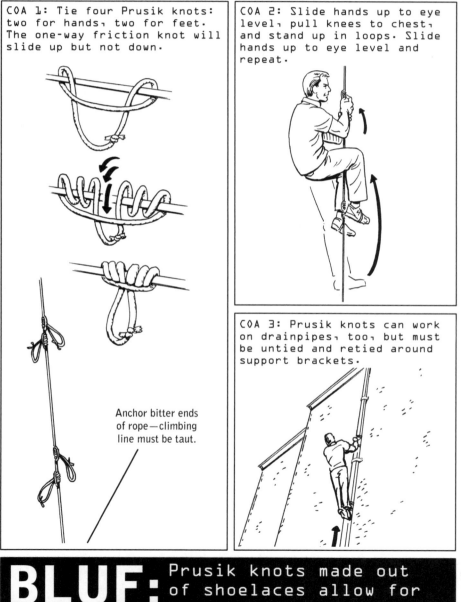

Anchor bitter ends of rope—climbing line must be taut.

BLUF: Prusik knots made out of shoelaces allow for emergency escapes.

When fitting into a particular region, a Nomad works through an environmental checklist, the first dimension of which is **personal**. How do his look and manner stack up to the environment? Travelers who look and act like fish out of water are prime targets for criminals of all stripes, and operatives who make themselves conspicuous are prime candidates for discovery.

The secondary dimension of this process is cultivating **cultural** awareness, which means constantly weighing actions and preferences against the prevailing cultural context. If the general population forgoes ketchup on their sandwiches or ice in their drinks, the operative will follow suit.

Next is **situational** awareness, meaning the operative continually scans his environment for potential dangers, playing out worst-case scenarios in order to identify which actions to take *before* crisis strikes. Within thirty seconds of having entered a restaurant, he has canvassed all exits and spotted any potential improvised weapons in the vicinity. He has also identified his "invisible thresholds," the imaginary lines whose crossing will spur him into swift, decisive action. If he spots an armed guard carrying an automatic weapon, he will quickly determine his "threshold" for escape or defensive action—i.e., should the guard look his way repeatedly, he will duck out the back door.

The final dimension of total awareness is **third-party** awareness. The operative is always keenly aware of anyone who might be watching *him*—whether he's operating in another country or using the Internet, his goal is to remain undetected by third parties such as law enforcement officials, citizens, criminals, and even hackers.

No. 017: Blend into Any Environment

CONOP: Understand and implement self-awareness in order to blend into any environment.

Personal Awareness

Cultural Awareness

Situational Awareness

Third-Party Awareness

BLUF: The environment should always dictate dress, mannerisms, and actions.

PART III

INFRASTRUCTURE DEVELOPMENT: LODGING, TRANSPORTATION, WEAPONS

018 Hotel Security and Safety Awareness

Hotel rooms are notoriously unsecure locations. Especially in developing nations, even trusted, name-brand properties can be susceptible to graft and surveillance—some of it officially sanctioned. In an era of global uncertainty, aggressive governments go to great lengths to collect intelligence on Westerners, whether they be high-ranking diplomats or run-of-the-mill businesspeople. Many travel blind in the face of these invisible threats, assuming they are safe when tucked away in their hotel rooms or rental cars. But any property controlled by an unknown entity is vulnerable to a multitude of threats.

Some hotels will actually place Westerners in rooms that are wired for surveillance. One way to thwart their efforts is to change rooms and hotels frequently. Because these properties are also subject to unexpected emergencies, the safest rooms are those on second or third floors. Most countries' fire services are not equipped to reach any higher—but a Nomad avoids the ground floor, as in the event of a hostile invasion, having some distance from the lobby is crucial. (Terrorists will most likely work their way up from the ground floor.)

An operative will look for a room that is equidistant from stairwells and elevators—a room too close to the emergency exit exposes him to the risk of being grabbed and shoved into a stairwell. Too far, and he is at a disadvantage when trying to make a speedy getaway.

Civilian BLUF: Hotels are targets for both common criminals and professional con men, and lobbies are particularly great places for criminals to stalk their prey without the risk of being challenged—the likelihood that they'll be questioned by hotel staff is low. Fortunately hotels have many entrances and exits; use them unpredictably to avoid creating routines that could be observed and anticipated.

No. 018: Hotel Security and Safety Awareness

CONOP: Understand hotel security and safety abroad.

COA 1: A column of rooms or an entire floor can be wired for concealed audio and video surveillance. Westerners are regularly pushed into rooms that are prewired for listening and watching.

COA 2: Request rooms on second or third floors: Most countries' fire services and truck ladders are not tall enough to reach any farther.

COA 3: Request rooms between fire exits and elevators, equidistant from escape routes. Rooms near the stairwells should be avoided as they provide advantages to abductors.

COA 4: Employ all means of exit. Use stairs and elevators evenly. Enter and exit hotel from different doors at random. A Nomad's hotel routine should be as irregular as his movement around town.

FIRE EXIT

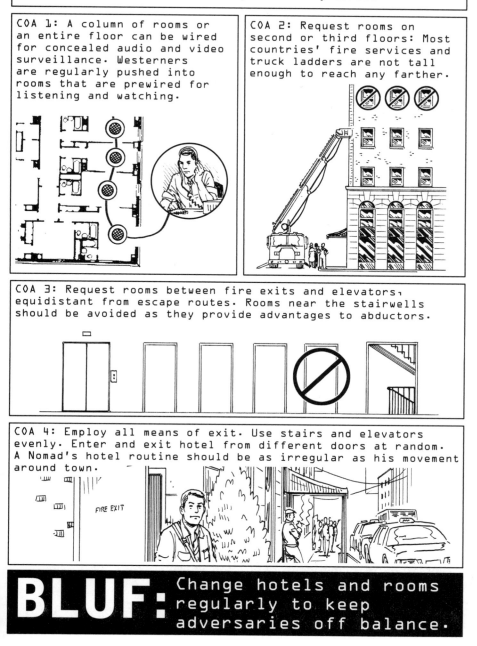

BLUF: Change hotels and rooms regularly to keep adversaries off balance.

019 Prevent a Hotel Room Invasion

Hotel guests can mitigate risk by making educated decisions about room and floor selection (see page 48). But hotel room door locks are notoriously flimsy, and even the most well-chosen room is only as secure as its doorframe, often a slim wooden structure bearing little to no reinforcement. So civilians traveling through particularly high-risk regions may wish to assess the layout of their rooms and construct additional fortifications.

While a solid lock provides a measure of protection against lock picking, only a reinforced doorframe can prevent an assailant from kicking in a door—a few strong blows will hammer a metal deadbolt right through a wooden frame. Covering the entire width of the door, an improvised door bar spreads the pressure of the blows along the bar, relieving the deadbolt of some of the impact and preventing it from bursting through the doorframe. Fastened with a pair of small eyelet screws, the reinforcement mechanism leaves behind only a minimal signature once it is removed.

In rooms where doors open outward (more common outside of the United States), invaders must pull the door, rather than kicking it, in order to force entry—a more difficult task to begin with. A simple trick makes their job even more challenging: running a length of nylon line from the doorknob to a fixed structure or to another closed, locked door.

In rooms where doors open inward, wedging or barricading the door will provide temporary reinforcement, giving an operative time to plan an escape route or create an improvised weapon while invaders struggle against the obstacles he has set in their path—from wooden wedges typically used to keep doors open to a lock reinforcement mechanism made out of a broomstick. As a method of last resort, piling a mass of furniture in front of the door provides an acceptable means of delaying attackers.

No. 019: Prevent a Hotel Room Invasion

CONOP: Control points of access using improvised barricades.

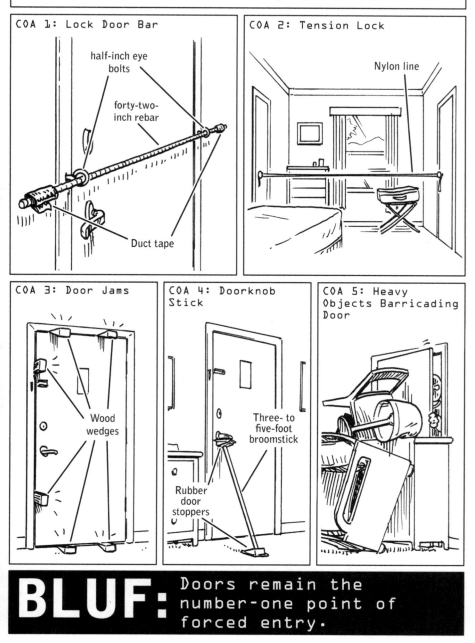

COA 1: Lock Door Bar

half-inch eye bolts

forty-two-inch rebar

Duct tape

COA 2: Tension Lock

Nylon line

COA 3: Door Jams

Wood wedges

COA 4: Doorknob Stick

Three- to five-foot broomstick

Rubber door stoppers

COA 5: Heavy Objects Barricading Door

BLUF: Doors remain the number-one point of forced entry.

020 Conceal Belongings within Lodging

When moving within the area of operation, operatives may take refuge in a hotel room (booked under an assumed name), but they never let their guard down—for they are always one room inspection away from discovery, and with it mission failure.

While it is best practice to carry or hide weapons and identification papers on their person or in the dead spaces of an operational vehicle, there are times when sensitive gear, tools, or data need to be securely stowed in a rented room. Hotel safes offer negligible protection, as they are frequently checked by hotel staff. Instead, operatives rely on elaborate hiding techniques well known to prison inmates the world over.

Successful concealment spots should be time-consuming for intruders to unearth. Intruders (and hotel staff alike) always move quickly when they're canvassing a room, as they're fearful of being intercepted. Hiding spots that involve screwdrivers (the back panel of a television, power sockets) will prove too time-intensive for most thieves to defeat. These spots will also betray traces of tampering—deliberately aligning the screws on an outlet or adjusting the rings on a shower curtain are measures that are sure to trump the average intruder.

Air vents are the perfect width for hiding laptops or tablets containing valuable information—just unscrew the grate and place them in the airshaft. Anything flat can be taped to the underside of a drawer.

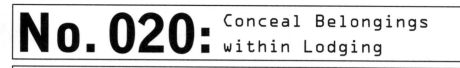

No. 020: Conceal Belongings within Lodging

CONOP: Conceal important documents, money, and digital media.

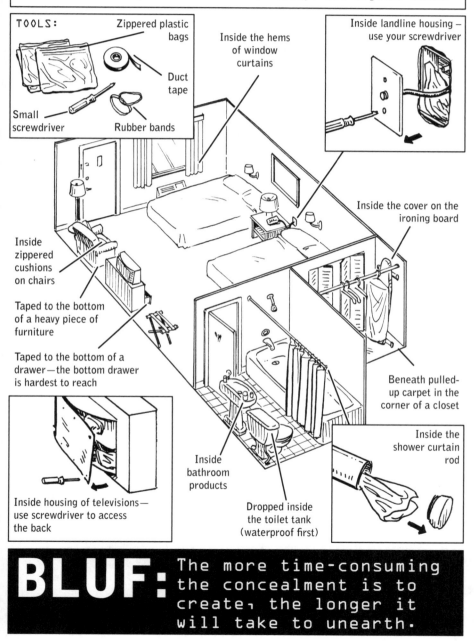

TOOLS:
- Zippered plastic bags
- Duct tape
- Small screwdriver
- Rubber bands

Inside the hems of window curtains

Inside landline housing — use your screwdriver

Inside the cover on the ironing board

Inside zippered cushions on chairs

Taped to the bottom of a heavy piece of furniture

Taped to the bottom of a drawer—the bottom drawer is hardest to reach

Beneath pulled-up carpet in the corner of a closet

Inside the shower curtain rod

Inside housing of televisions—use screwdriver to access the back

Inside bathroom products

Dropped inside the toilet tank (waterproof first)

BLUF: The more time-consuming the concealment is to create, the longer it will take to unearth.

021 Build a Room Hide

Collecting long-term intelligence on a target is a process that could go on for many days and weeks—pinning down the target's daily routines and establishing vulnerabilities over time is key to effective surveillance. But sitting in a parked car for days on end is bound to arouse suspicion in even the most anonymous of cities. For long-term stakeouts the operative must create a room "hide," an indoor base from which to collect intelligence unobserved.

The best room is one that provides an unobstructed line of sight over the surveillance target. An upper floor will maximize an operative's field of view while minimizing his visibility. (Most civilians don't lift their gaze above eye level as they go about their daily lives.) Before building his hide, the operative surveys the outside of the building during the day and at night. If curtains in the building are drawn or shut by maid service at certain times of the day, the operative follows suit.

While collection by night assures a certain level of discretion, daytime surveillance may yield more valuable information. To collect unobserved, the operative shields the room from view by building a virtual cloak of invisibility: a temporary darkroom that will enable him to disappear behind a window in broad daylight. Instead of reflecting light as white walls do, its dark curtains will absorb light, reducing visibility in the room without compromising the look of the window, which will appear no different than any other when viewed from a ground-level vantage point. Pinning the sheets to the ceiling in a double layer will prevent light from leaking into the darkroom upon entry and exit.

No. 021: Build a Room Hide

CONOP: Construct urban hide site for static surveillance operations.

COA 1: Choose a window with best field of view of target.

Always choose window higher than target.

Observe window dressing, etc., to ensure hide window looks like others.

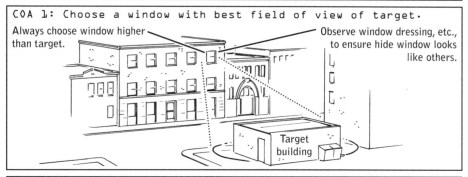

Target building

COA 2: Tack five black or dark-colored sheets to ceiling, creating a three-sided room around window. Hang fourth and fifth sheets two to three feet behind back sheet—this will prevent backlighting when entering/exiting hide site.

Create a darkroom within the room.

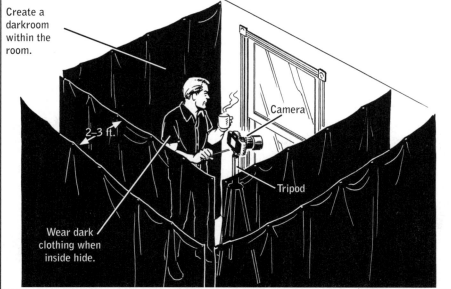

2–3 ft.

Camera

Tripod

Wear dark clothing when inside hide.

BLUF: Through proper light discipline and camouflage, invisibility is achievable.

022 Steal a Vehicle

Unlike their big-screen counterparts, Violent Nomads don't drive Aston Martins, Porsches, or any other type of Bond-worthy rides. The best vehicle for carrying out a mission is the vehicle that attracts the least attention—the vehicle that will allow an operative to tail and sit on a target for hours without risking detection. The vehicle that will blend into the flow of traffic after a quick getaway.

Violent Nomads often rent, cash-purchase, or commandeer vehicles; prepare and modify them for a mission; and then dump them when they are no longer needed. Stolen vehicles don't leave a paper trail—and even though the Nomad will always use false identification and credit cards, he prefers to avoid leaving behind any potential traces. The vehicle can be used operationally, and then dumped or burned long before it is reported missing.

Selecting a Vehicle
The optimal vehicle for any mission is the one that is unremarkable in every sense. This will be dependent upon the setting of the mission, so Nomads carefully survey their operational environments to determine the best car for the job. They select a make, model, and color that mirror the most popular choices in the area. Beyond the type of car, details are significant. If locals in the area of operation hang miniature country flags from their rearview mirrors, the Nomad will follow suit.

Additional considerations for identifying an operational vehicle include:

Dead Space and Voids: The environment and/or particularities of a mission may dictate a vehicle with plenty of voids where operational gear and weapons can be concealed. A surveillance mission may require cameras, and a mission in a desert or other secluded environment may require stocking enough food and water for days. Vehicles with the most usable space include sedans, SUVs, and utility vehicles.

No. 022: Steal a Vehicle

CONOP: Commandeer a vehicle for operational use.

COA 1: Valet Key/Car Theft

COA 2: Carjacking

COA 3: Look for Hidden Keys

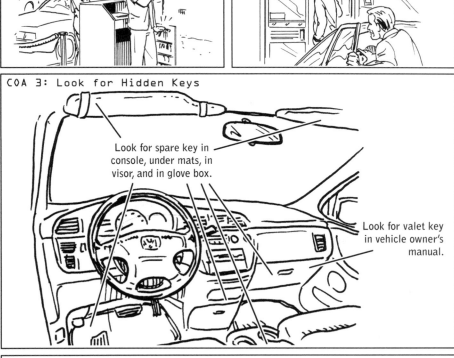

Look for spare key in console, under mats, in visor, and in glove box.

Look for valet key in vehicle owner's manual.

COA 4: Steal a Honda (1999 models or older)

Break plastic housing on steering column.

Break steering column lock by pulling on steering wheel in one direction with brute force.

Separate lock cylinder from lock body. Insert screwdriver and turn. This turns the solenoid and starts the car.

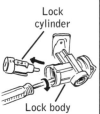

Lock cylinder

Lock body

BLUF: The fastest way to acquire a car is to steal one that is already running.

Condition: Marks, dents, or scrapes are conspicuous attributes that third parties might notice and transmit to authorities. Conversely, cars that look too clean also risk attracting notice. In most environments outside wealthy enclaves, a soiled car will have a better chance of blending in with the rest of the cars on the road.

Stealing a Vehicle

The sophisticated kill switches, transponders, and other security features now inherent to most modern vehicles make car theft a much more complex proposition than it once was; in order to get a car to start, a key needs to be both cut to the ignition and embedded with the right transponder. This is why Nomads and common car thieves alike seek out opportunities to nab car keys, carjack running vehicles, and hack their way into older-model cars with less stringent security features.

Valet and daily parking structures tend to display extremely lax security measures. Keys are often simply tagged and placed in unlocked drawers at valet booths that are frequently left unattended, providing Nomads with an opportunity to quickly and easily filch a set of car keys to the model of their choice.

Nomads may also canvass the streets, seizing opportunities for carjacking as they arise. Civilians frequently render themselves vulnerable by leaving their keys in the ignition as they withdraw cash from an ATM or settle the gas bill inside the station.

When it comes to stealing a car the old-fashioned way, Nomads seek out older-model vehicles with proven security vulnerabilities—Hondas being one reliable example. Once the lock cylinder is bypassed, the ignition on these models is easily switched on by the tip of a screwdriver.

Their first order of business is searching for spare keys and "valet keys," the thin keys many automakers embed into vehicles' owner's manuals; these allow access to doors and ignition but won't open trunks or glove compartments. Even high-performance vehicles have their particular vulnerabilities, and Nomads are keen students in this area. Certain BMW models have wiring harnesses by their trunks that can be shorted and used to unlock the entire vehicle.

To expose the lock cylinder on an older-model vehicle (see diagram), they use a few hard knocks with the handle of a screwdriver to break the plastic housing on the steering column. Then, they use the same technique to disengage the lock cylinder from the lock body.

Before the operative starts the engine, he must also bypass the steering column lock—a very simple lock mechanism that can be broken by yanking the wheel in any one direction with brute force. Inserting the tip of the screwdriver into the lock body and turning it to the right is all it takes to start the engine.

Civilian BLUF: Never leave a running car unattended, even for a moment. Never leave your car keys in your vehicle, even in a locked garage. Check your owner's manual for a valet key and move it to a safe place.

023 Operational Vehicle Prep

Once an operational vehicle has been acquired, undertaking a range of adjustments will enhance performance and decrease visibility and traceability. These may include:

- Commandeering voids and dead space such as the dashboard on the passenger's side, airbag compartments, door panels, and seat covers—a suite of caches well known to drug smugglers and mules. In a surveillance or combat context, these spaces can hold anything from a rifle to a life-support system containing water, food, money, laptops, and other communication devices.
- Outfitting the vehicle with forged license plates and registration documentation. Expired tags might blow a Nomad's cover in the event that he is pulled over.
- Installing a nanny cam disguised in a tissue box on the rear dash as an extra set of eyes. Depending on the direction in which it is trained, the camera can be used for surveillance or to determine if someone is following the vehicle.
- Disabling daytime running lights, brake lights, and interior lights and chimes for inconspicuous travel. Partially pull interior lightbulbs out of their sockets—far enough to prevent them from turning on, but not so far that they will dangle and attract attention in the event that the operative is pulled over.
- Overinflating tires for optimal performance.

No. 023: Operational Vehicle Prep

CONOP: Prepare a vehicle for operational use.

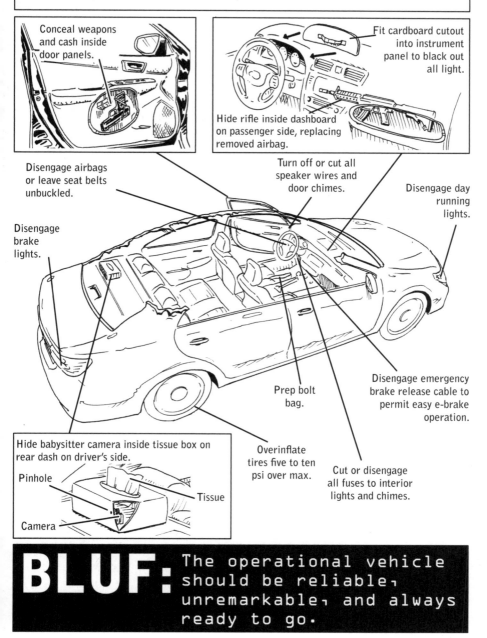

Conceal weapons and cash inside door panels.

Fit cardboard cutout into instrument panel to black out all light.

Hide rifle inside dashboard on passenger side, replacing removed airbag.

Disengage airbags or leave seat belts unbuckled.

Turn off or cut all speaker wires and door chimes.

Disengage day running lights.

Disengage brake lights.

Disengage emergency brake release cable to permit easy e-brake operation.

Prep bolt bag.

Hide babysitter camera inside tissue box on rear dash on driver's side.

Pinhole

Tissue

Camera

Overinflate tires five to ten psi over max.

Cut or disengage all fuses to interior lights and chimes.

BLUF: The operational vehicle should be reliable, unremarkable, and always ready to go.

024 Escape and Evasion Vehicle Prep

Due to their high inherent risk, escape and evasion driving techniques are used by operatives only in cases of extreme urgency, in vehicles that have been specially chosen and retrofitted to make maneuvers such as the J-turn or the Reverse 180 (pages 220 and 222) possible. High-center-of-gravity vehicles such as SUVs are prone to flipping, while smaller cars might not fare as well in collisions. Examples of retrofitting include:

Selecting Tires: Tires should be replaced with high-performance models inflated to the recommended pounds per square inch.

Seat-Belt Workaround: In a car that is flipped upside down, the seat belt's pendulum locking system could become a deadly liability. If the weight of the operative's body swings the pendulum deep into the car door, the belt may lock into place and lose its ability to unbuckle, so a well-placed razor blade can be a lifesaving measure.

Airbag Disengagement: The last thing a Nomad wants is airbags going off—and in newer vehicle models, automatically killing the engine as they deploy—during a high-speed pursuit.

Left-Foot Braking: The human nervous system functions faster and more efficiently when both sides of the body work together—which is why race car drivers and operatives use the left foot for braking and the right for gas.

Threshold Braking: Learning to depress the brake pedal without locking up the tires is necessary for precise handling. When deployed at a high speed, this controlled braking maneuver enables an operative to come to a stop with minimal sliding or skidding.

No. 024: Escape and Evasion Vehicle Prep

CONOP: Prepare a vehicle for high-speed chases.

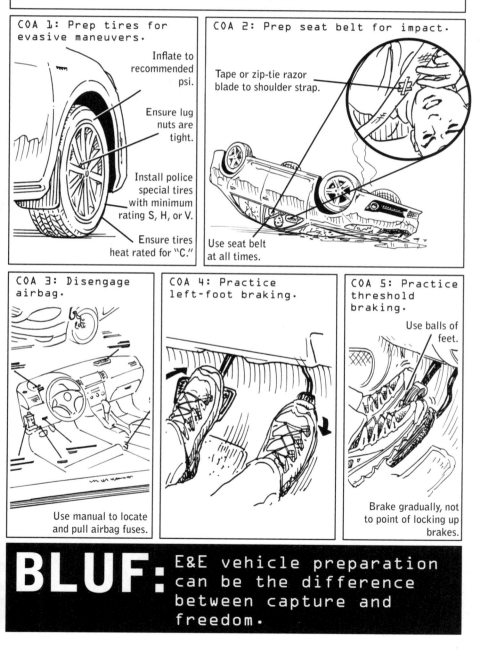

COA 1: Prep tires for evasive maneuvers.

Inflate to recommended psi.

Ensure lug nuts are tight.

Install police special tires with minimum rating S, H, or V.

Ensure tires heat rated for "C."

COA 2: Prep seat belt for impact.

Tape or zip-tie razor blade to shoulder strap.

Use seat belt at all times.

COA 3: Disengage airbag.

Use manual to locate and pull airbag fuses.

COA 4: Practice left-foot braking.

COA 5: Practice threshold braking.

Use balls of feet.

Brake gradually, not to point of locking up brakes.

BLUF: E&E vehicle preparation can be the difference between capture and freedom.

025 Build a Vehicle Hide

The optimal hide site for static surveillance is a room with a view, but in some cases Nomads are forced to set up temporary hide sites inside their vehicles. This scenario involves a slew of vulnerabilities and discomforts, but exposure can be mitigated by the construction of a sheet-based darkroom similar to what an operative would build in an urban hide site (page 54). Such a darkroom allows him to disappear as if behind the darkest of tinted glass—but unlike glass, it does not leave him vulnerable to bright sunshine and curious onlookers.

A large sedan or SUV with tinted windows and folding seats gives the operative the ability to set up a full-fledged surveillance suite inside his low-tech darkroom. A tripod, an SLR camera, and a shutter release cable will produce higher-quality night shots than those captured by specialized night vision equipment.

To avoid being given away by engine noise, running lights, or exhaust fumes, the operative always turns off the ignition. In cold weather, he applies Rain-X to interior glass and wears a nonporous jacket that retains body heat in order to prevent windows from fogging up. He uses empty bottles as receptacles for urine; when filled and capped these can be placed on the front or rear dash to act as defrosting devices.

To enter the darkroom, he will construct a pretext for leaving the vehicle momentarily, such as going to the corner for a cup of coffee. Returning to the car, he quickly and casually slips into the back door on the driver's side—to most onlookers it will look like someone has just settled into the driver's seat.

No. 025: Build a Vehicle Hide

CONOP: Construct a vehicle hide site for mobile surveillance.

COA 1: Acquire two black sheets, safety pins, and scissors. Cut sheets in half to create four panels.

Hang panels to create a hide in rear portion of car.

Safety pins will adhere panels to fabric head lining.

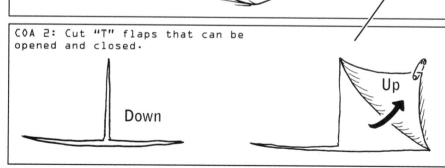

Use scissors to cut self-sealing observation ports.

COA 2: Cut "T" flaps that can be opened and closed.

Down

Up

BLUF: Vehicle hides are only as good as the vehicle's ability to blend into the environment.

026 Steal a Plane

Most civilians would be very surprised to learn that, for those in possession of flight training, swiping the world's most common aircraft—a Cessna 152 or 172—is no more difficult than picking the lock on a flimsy office desk. But for a Nomad looking to perform aerial surveillance or cross borders undetected (see page 32), stealing small, privately owned planes is just another means of securing an untraceable method of transportation.

Relatively quiet, fuel-efficient, and reliable, single small-engine planes have several advantages for Nomads. They are high-wing (as opposed to low-wing) aircraft—which means their wings won't get in the way if an operative needs to jump out in a hurry. Another significant advantage is defined by the acronym STOAL, for "Short Takeoff and Landing": Small aircraft do not require very much space in which to take off and land, which enables Nomads to avoid runways and instead land in open fields and other deserted spaces.

Most important, small aircraft tend to be outfitted with flimsy, highly vulnerable wafer locks, making them extremely easy for an operative to steal using the picking tools and techniques that apply to any common door locks (page 110).

Small aircraft are typically kept at single-run airports, where security is negligible and airspace goes unmonitored by transportation or customs authorities. Once an operative has broken into the plane, he will likely be able to take off and fly away without attracting any notice.

Civilian BLUF: Owners of private planes are well advised to store their planes in hangars and/or lock them down like bicycles.

No. 026: Steal a Plane

CONOP: Commandeer an airplane for operational use.

COA 1: Pick the door locks.

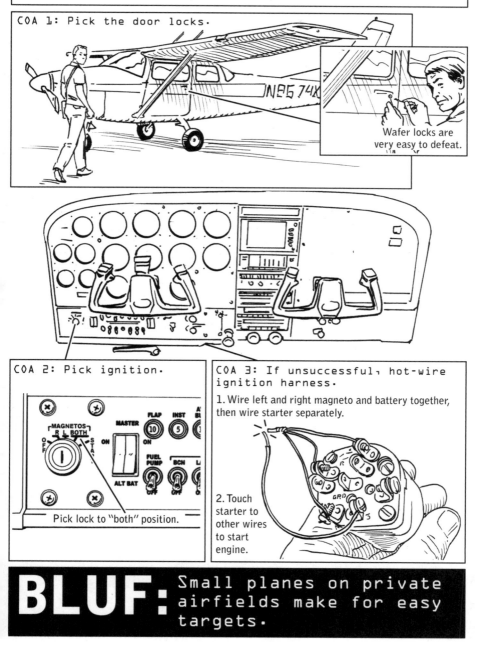

Wafer locks are very easy to defeat.

COA 2: Pick ignition.

Pick lock to "both" position.

COA 3: If unsuccessful, hot-wire ignition harness.

1. Wire left and right magneto and battery together, then wire starter separately.

2. Touch starter to other wires to start engine.

BLUF: Small planes on private airfields make for easy targets.

IMPROVISED WEAPONS

Violent Nomads are always prepared for the eventuality of being captured and stripped of their weapons—or that, in a given context, even a well-concealed weapon will pose too great a risk of detection. But because they are well versed in turning everyday items into improvised weapons, they will never truly be caught unaware.

There is no such thing as the ideal improvised weapon, as the best weapon in any scenario is simply the one that can be reached when it is needed. If it can be easily acquired within the area of operation and carried without arousing suspicion, all the better.

Though improvisation rules the roost, some effective weapons of self-defense can be created with a minimum of advance planning.

For civilians, learning to see the danger inherent in everyday objects has multiple benefits. A man holding a tightly rolled newspaper may be a perpetrator getting ready to strike, but only those with the foresight to recognize his weapon will be prepared to fend off his assault. And in the event of an attack, the civilian who is able to recognize the self-defense potential in the materials at hand will be one step ahead.

Civilian BLUF: While the examples used in the following pages describe operatives repurposing everyday items in the course of a mission, many innocuous everyday items can stand in as improvised weapons of self-defense as the situation demands. Even salt and pepper shakers, found on restaurant tables all over the world, can be used to temporarily blind an assailant—thrown into an opponent's eyes, they create a momentary stinging and/or blinding effect that may give you the time to escape or gain the upper hand.

027 Make a Water Bottle Silencer

Gunfire's two biggest giveaways are sparks and sound: an extremely loud bang as the gunpowder inside the bullet's cartridge is ignited, along with the resulting flash. But paired with subsonic bullets from a .22-caliber or .45-caliber pistol, an improvised silencer can eliminate both. Though some states restrict or outright ban the purchase of silencers and suppressors, a viable alternative can be made from a plastic water bottle, a square of fine wire mesh, and a stainless steel scouring sponge. The only audible noise will be a ticking sound, the result of the pistol's hammer initiating the blow by striking the primer.

Mimicking the action of a standard silencer—a perforated steel tube encased within a solid steel tube—the improvised version uses a two-pronged muffling device. Rolled into a tight cylindrical shape, the stiff layer of steel mesh will hold its form and direct the bullet through and out of the water bottle in a straight line. Tugging on the scouring sponge will help it expand to fill the rest of the space in the bottle, creating a metal pillow that traps and muffles sound. Like a makeshift steel box, the contraption dampens sound and light waves with a surprising degree of effectiveness.

Civilian BLUF: For an imaginative predator, lethal materials are readily available. Stainless steel scourers can be obtained at any grocery or hardware store, and fine wire mesh can be cut out of window screens or screen doors. Awareness is key.

No. 027: Make a Water Bottle Silencer

CONOP: Construct a disposable silencer from a water bottle.

COA 1: Acquire materials.

Water bottle

Stainless steel scourer

Fine wire mesh (stainless or aluminum)

COA 2: Prep bottle.

Cut off bottle end; drill or cut hole at center.

COA 3: Roll steel mesh into cylinder that fits snugly into mouth of bottle.

Cardboard or tape wrapped around mesh to tighten fit

COA 4: Assemble silencer.

Tape bottle back together.

Fill bottle with scourer.

COA 5: Attach to weapon.

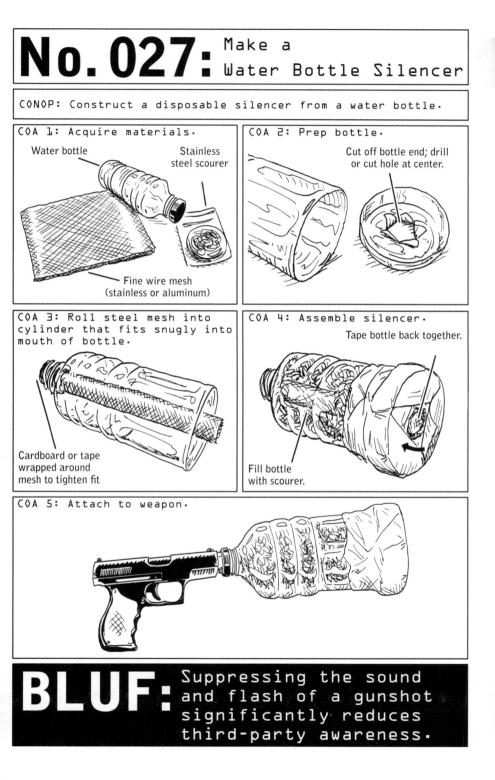

BLUF: Suppressing the sound and flash of a gunshot significantly reduces third-party awareness.

028 Transform an Umbrella into a Lead Pipe

Because bullets and bullet holes leave forensic traces behind, the world's most common assassination weapon is neither a rifle nor a handgun but a piece of common lead pipe concealed in newspaper. A dense and heavy sap leaves behind only its intended effect: crushed bone and, if applied to a human skull, utter annihilation.

Reinforced with lead, a collapsible umbrella has also been used by criminals to the same effect. To turn one into a weapon of self-defense, acquire three to four heavy-duty wrenches. Slide the wrenches under the canopy and around the handle, zip-tying them to the umbrella handle before securing the outside of the weapon with additional zip ties. Black ties on a black umbrella will not be visible—which means that the weapon will look no different from an ordinary umbrella (though it will be significantly heavier and is not recommended for everyday use).

No. 028: Transform an Umbrella into a Lead Pipe

CONOP: Load a standard umbrella with metal wrenches to create a lethal weapon.

COA 1: Acquire an umbrella, zip ties, and three or four wrenches.

COA 2: Load the wrenches into the umbrella.

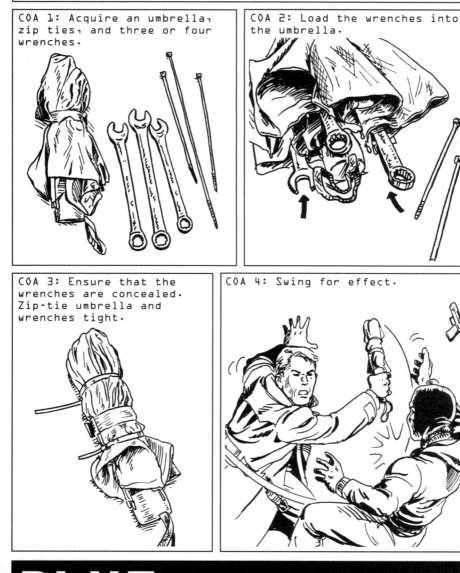

COA 3: Ensure that the wrenches are concealed. Zip-tie umbrella and wrenches tight.

COA 4: Swing for effect.

BLUF: What appears innocent frequently is not.

029 Turn a Pen into a Weapon

The smartest pen is not a personal computing accessory but a deadly and completely inconspicuous weapon of self-defense. In a pinch, any pen grasped from the bottom of a handbag or briefcase can be used to inflict harm on an assailant, but one partiuclar make is especially effective: With a barrel made of 100 percent stainless steel, Zebra's original steel pen can moonlight as an incredible makeshift stabbing tool strong enough to pierce plywood.

To strike, hold the pen in a tight fist. Use an overhand grip to strike an assailant's head and an underhand grip if striking the throat or knee at close range.

No. 029: Turn a Pen into a Weapon

CONOP: Purchase and use pens to fight off adversaries.

COA 1: Carry steel-barreled Zebra F-400 or F-700 writing pens in bags and pockets, and stash them in vehicles and rooms.

COA 2: Overhand grip-allows penetration through plywood or for striking the head.

COA 3: Underhand grip-for striking throat or knee.

BLUF: The pen is mightier than the sword.

030 Use a Fishing Weight as an Improvised Sap

The innocent trappings of a fishing trip, an eight-ounce fishing weight and a bandana would attract no notice in a traveler's backpack. Seen separately, the items pose no discernible threat. But in the face of imminent danger, they can be turned into an effective, small, and dense makeshift sap.

Fold the weight into the bandana, then roll the bandana into a cylinder. Fold the two ends together and strike opponents, aiming for knee (to cause buckling) or head (to cause the assailant to lose consciousness). The resulting weapon will be powerful enough to crack a coconut and do equivalent damage to a human skull.

No. 030: Use a Fishing Weight as an Improvised Sap

CONOP: Combine a bandana and eight-ounce fishing weight to create a lethal sap.

COA 1: Lay out bandana square and place fishing weight in the center.

COA 2: Fold bandana diagonally.

COA 3: Roll bandana from apex to base.

COA 4: Fold end to end and swing for effect.

Coconuts are ten times harder than a human skull.

BLUF: When used in tandem, two innocuous items can become devastating.

031 Make a Flexible Chain Weapon

Though now most closely identified with the world of motorcycle gangs, chain weapons have been in use for a very long time. Modeled after the medieval weapon called a chain mace, a basic flexible chain weapon can be made by attaching two items that naturally belong together (and hence should attract no suspicion): a chain and a padlock. The resulting weapon will be strong enough to crack human bone.

Though any bicyclist can use his chain and lock as improvised weapons of self-defense, the ideal length of chain—slightly longer than an average forearm—is shorter than that used to lock up a bike. An overlong chain will swing too slowly, giving an assailant plenty of time to react.

No. 031: Make a Flexible Chain Weapon

CONOP: Construct a heavy-duty weapon for use in hand-to-hand combat.

COA 1: Acquire a chain and padlock.

COA 2: Cut chain down to arm's length. Lock padlock to one end of chain.

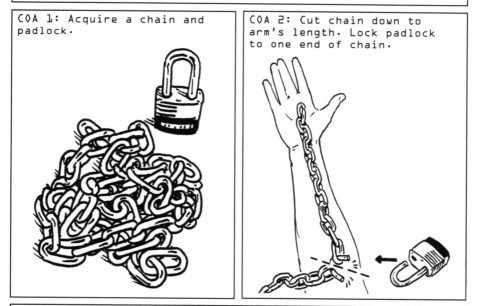

COA 3: Use the padlock end to strike the target.

BLUF: Chains and locks can be carried through security without hassle.

032 Make a Newspaper Nail Bat

The sight of a person walking down the street holding a newspaper is one so common and unremarkable that in the surveillance world, newspapers are frequently used as decoys; like cell phones or cigarettes, they present operatives with an alibi for loitering on park benches while surveying a target, a means of becoming a creature of their environment. In a pinch, they can also be used as a weapon.

Rolled up into a tight cylinder that is doubled over onto itself and taped together, a few sheets of newspaper become a surprisingly sturdy baton. Wetting the paper gives the baton a significant amount of extra weight, and the addition of a two-and-a-half-inch wood nail turns the baton into a potentially devastating bludgeon.

Civilian BLUF: In a volatile, unsecured environment, even the most innocent of props can be cause for alarm.

No. 032: Make a Newspaper Nail Bat

CONOP: Roll a newspaper into a damaging striking weapon.

COA 1: Acquire materials (newspaper, nails, duct tape).

COA 2: Use wet paper for extra weight. Roll paper tightly.

COA 3: Fold rolled paper and unfold. Insert nail just right or left of fold. Fold again so that nail is pointing outward.

COA 4: Tape top and bottom of nail bat together.

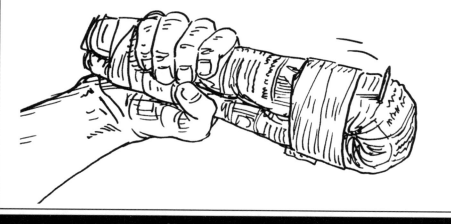

BLUF: Newspapers and nails can be found everywhere in the world.

033 Deploy a Roll of Coins

For an easy-to-reach advantage in hand-to-hand combat, an operative keeps a roll of coins in his pocket at all times. (Foreign currency closest in size to American nickels or quarters will result in optimal heft.) Gripped in the center of the palm, the coins will increase the density and weight of his fist—a street-fighting trick that will significantly amplify the velocity and impact of a power punch such as a straight right or left punch, a hook, or an uppercut.

Stuffed into a sock, pillowcase, or handkerchief, that same roll of coins can be used as an improvised sap. This type of weapon gains a surprising amount of power from a combination of velocity and density. When swung with force, it can break bones; directed at an opponent's head, the impact can easily result in a knockout.

In its bloodiest incarnation, a roll of coins can be studded with household nails to create a sharp and deadly version of brass knuckles. A punch with these spiked knuckles (another hallmark of street fighting) will inflict serious and unexpected damage no matter where it lands.

Carried separately, each of these items—a roll of coins, a few stray nails, a pair of socks—is non-alerting. But when a Nomad senses danger ahead, they can be assembled into effective options for self-defense in under a minute's time.

No. 033: Deploy a Roll of Coins

CONOP: Turn an innocent roll of coins into an effective weapon of self-defense.

COA 1: Increase fist density: Clinch a roll of coins in punching fist.

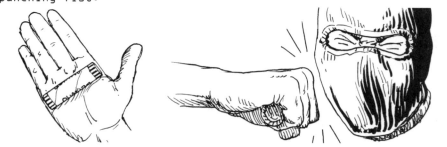

COA 2: Make an improvised sap: Place roll of coins in a sock and swing at head of adversary.

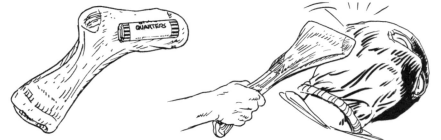

COA 3: Make a set of spiked knuckles: Push three nails, finger width apart, through roll.

Several coins will need to be removed; pack the rest tightly around nails.

BLUF: Coins can be used for tolls, meters, public transportation, and to crush a face.

PART IV

SURVEILLANCE: OBSERVATION, TRACKING, AND COUNTER-SURVEILLANCE

034 Dismounted Surveillance

Stalking a subject on foot may be a low-tech proposition, but it is also a complex endeavor with a high inherent risk of discovery. Conducting surveillance alone is particularly difficult, the stress of potentially being "burned" amplified as patience and stamina are tested over long hours and days. Because an operative can't switch out with team members, he is more likely to be spotted by the target.

Several rules of thumb can mitigate risk. When on foot, remain in the target's blind spot at all times. While the target eats, sleeps, or works, take the opportunity to change clothes. Switch out of clothing as often as possible—at a distance, human beings are recognized by the color and style of their clothing rather than their facial features. Never wear the same thing twice.

Use the environment to gain advantage. Glass surfaces offer reflective capabilities and can also allow an operative to scan the street from a potected vantage point.

Vary the timing of surveillance to learn the target's patterns while thwarting possible countersurveillance. Do not attempt to follow the target all day, every day—that's a surefire way to arouse suspicion. Around-the-clock surveillance is better suited for a multimember team with plenty of people who can rotate in and out.

Eighty-five percent of surveillance teams are detected by third parties rather than by the targets themselves—which underlines the importance of blending into the environment. Look the part, and carry books, maps, cigarettes, and other forms of "pocket litter" as non-alerting excuses for loitering.

No. 034: Dismounted Surveillance

CONOP: Conduct surveillance on foot without detection.

COA 1: Stay out of target's field of view (FOV).

Walk in blind spots.

FIELD OF VIEW

Anticipate target looking around when crossing streets; duck inside when possible.

COA 2: Change clothes often.

Messenger bag/backpack

Alternate lights and darks.

Shoes/flip-flops

COA 3: Use glass when possible.

Observe from inside.

Use reflections.

COA 4: Vary time and days of surveillance.

COA 5: Carry items that provide an excuse for being static.

Loose change for buses, meters, vending machines, etc.

Cigarettes, gum, or glasses that need cleaning

Books, newspapers, maps, etc.

BLUF: Be a creature of the environment and always have a reason to loiter.

Volatile, high-speed car chases may light up the silver screen, but the slow-paced reality of vehicular surveillance is defined by patience and persistence. It's easy to become complacent when stuck in bumper-to-bumper traffic or waiting outside a movie theater for two hours—and to lose sight of the "rabbit's" vehicle as he pulls a quick right or slips out of a parking lot during one of those momentary lapses in attention. Vigilance is key.

It's also surprisingly easy to be spotted when following a target too closely. To avoid detection, stay out of the target's mirrors and lane and remain one car behind at all times. Always observe the "two-turn limit." Following the target for more than two consecutive turns brings a serious risk of being burned. In this and many other regards, mounted surveillance is far better suited to a multi-member team in which one member can blow past a turn, letting the next surveillance team member take over and become the new "eye."

Avoid mirroring the target's actions, particularly on U-turns. If the target takes a U-turn, move to the next turn pocket, then turn around and catch up. Don't follow a rabbit through a series of odd maneuvers such as stairstepping through neighborhoods or pulling into dead ends; the rabbit is probably performing these maneuvers in order to confirm that he's being followed.

Let density determine distance. Stay close in dense traffic and/or urban environments with many stoplights. Two or three cars between an operative and the target could spell a loss if the operative misses a light or two because a car ahead of him has stopped to take a turn. In a rural area with low density, stay far back; fewer drivers on the road means less camouflage.

Civilian BLUF: Increase your awareness of cars that seem to be mirroring you as you drive (particularly those that follow you on multiple turns) and you will decrease your vulnerability to abductions or carjackings.

No. 035: Mobile Surveillance

CONOP: Conduct mobile surveillance without detection.

COA 1: Stay out of target's lane and mirrors and remain one car behind.

COA 2: Observe the two-turn limit: After two consecutive turns with the target, break off for the day.

COA 3: Never mirror target's actions (changing lanes, making turns and stops).

COA 4: Stop following after odd maneuvers: U-turns, stairstepping through neighborhoods, dead ends, and multiple stops between home and work.

COA 5: Density determines distance. Lots of cars, lots of buildings? Distance to target can be close. Rural, open roads, few vehicles? Stay very far away or disengage.

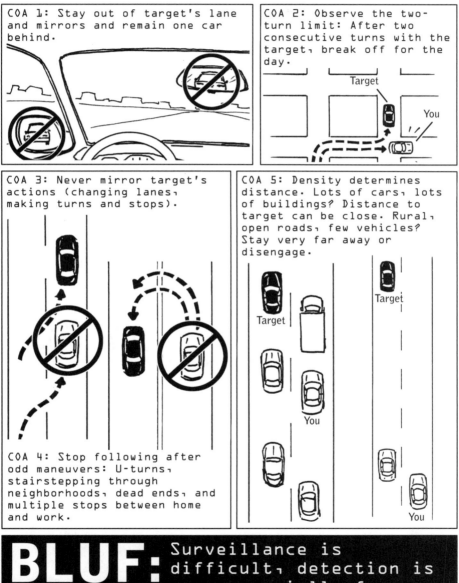

BLUF: Surveillance is difficult, detection is easy—especially for an operative working alone.

036 Make an Improvised Infrared Light

An operative collecting intelligence from inside a target's home or place of business may wait for days for the coast to clear—and when that moment arrives, his collection process must be swift and undetectable. In the dark of night, when even the smallest amount of ambient light can compromise a mission, an infrared light source provides an ideal recourse. Invisible to the naked eye, it allows a Nomad to search a room in complete darkness.

Though infrared bulbs and filters are commercially available, such purchases may create unwanted scrutiny; an improvised solution, using a flashlight, a piece of camera film or the slip of plastic inside floppy disks, and a camera phone, provides the same results.

While both film and floppy disks are becoming extinct in the developed world, they are still readily available in many countries. Placed in front of the flashlight's bulb, the film acts as a filter, blocking the flashlight's visible light rays to undetectable levels. A standard camera phone (see below for exceptions) will allow an operative to view the objects lit by the infrared beam emitting from his modified flashlight. Though he'll be working in complete darkness, any object the light is shining on will be visible in his camera monitor.

Note: Some of the newest camera phones come equipped with infrared blocking filters that render them unsuitable for this usage. To find out if a particular model will work, obtain a remote control. Turn the camera on and point the front end of the remote (the end with the LED lightbulbs built into it) toward the phone's screen. Press any button on the remote and look at it through the screen. If the camera *does* detect infrared light, the glow of the remote's LED bulbs will be visible. If not, an inexpensive phone purchased within the area of operation will be likely to include an infrared filter.

CONOP: Search a room in total darkness.

COA 1: Acquire flashlight and camera film.

COA 2: Trace lens of flashlight onto segment of film and cut out.

COA 3: Place film between lens and bulb.

BLUF: Improvised infrared lights can be used to land aircraft, track bad guys, and signal for help.

037 Make a Tracking Device for Night Surveillance

Mobile surveillance is a uniquely challenging skill set in the intelligence-gathering arsenal. Requiring a Nomad to engage with multiple streams of information at once—from the flow of traffic to a target's sudden turns to the possibility of being spotted—it becomes even more difficult if a vehicle's distinguishing features are eclipsed by the dark of night, when identifying a car by its make and model becomes a near impossibility. Similar difficulties emerge if a Nomad needs to track a target through dense urban environments or when the target drives a common vehicle in a country where license plates are seen as optional.

When the ever-present possibility of losing the target is multiplied by these factors, a rudimentary infrared tracking device can be used to illuminate the tracked vehicle. Forged out of camera film or floppy-disc material and a white-light keychain LED flashlight, it functions identically to an improvised infrared light (page 90). But instead of being handheld, once the device is assembled it is zip-tied to the undercarriage of the target vehicle.

Camera film or floppy-disc material will subtract the visible rays from any mechanism that emits white light, acting as a barrier that lets only infrared rays (invisible to the naked eye) through. Lending a telltale glow that is visible only to the Nomad viewing the roadway through the lens of a digital camera or smartphone, the resulting makeshift device provides the sort of close-range confirmation tracking that a satellite device (see page 100) might miss by several feet. (More suitable for longer-term surveillance, GPS tracking devices enable surveillance teams to establish the target's pattern of life over time.)

No. 037: Make a Tracking Device for Night Surveillance

CONOP: Construct infrared illuminators visible only through cameras, in order to track target vehicle at night.

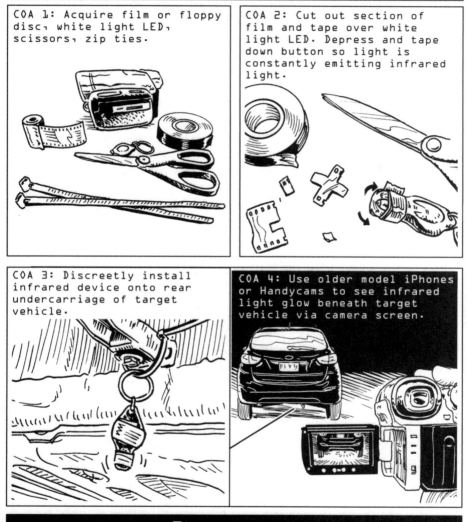

COA 1: Acquire film or floppy disc, white light LED, scissors, zip ties.

COA 2: Cut out section of film and tape over white light LED. Depress and tape down button so light is constantly emitting infrared light.

COA 3: Discreetly install infrared device onto rear undercarriage of target vehicle.

COA 4: Use older model iPhones or Handycams to see infrared light glow beneath target vehicle via camera screen.

BLUF: The cover of darkness provides advantages and disadvantages—aim to enhance the former and decrease the latter.

038 Detect Tampering of Personal Effects

Scrutiny of Westerners in developing economies is an increasingly common phenomenon. Whether seeking trade or government secrets or attempting to determine a visitor's ulterior motives for travel, in many countries hotel security and government officials work in tandem to surreptitiously police foreigners staying in their properties.

To find out if their belongings have been tampered with and determine their surveillance status, operatives use discreet alignment techniques to monitor the placement of electronics and valuables.

The key word is *discreet*. Giving host-nation security services reason to believe that an operative is onto them could result in their upping the ante and moving to detain him—or worse.

Cardinal Bearings Technique: Use a compass or a compass app to align items in cardinal directions. Position obstructions around the USB ports on a laptop to determine whether intruders have used flash drives to download data.

Space and Depth Technique: Experienced hackers will bypass the operating system, flipping a laptop upside down and unscrewing the hard drive in order to capture the contents of the computer. To determine whether a laptop has been moved, use a thumb as a measurement tool when setting it into position.

Traps: The "do not disturb" sign on a hotel door can be put to good use as a telltale sign that a room has, in fact, been disturbed.

Photo Trap: Use Photo Trap or a similar app (see page 126) to compare before and after shots of belongings. Such apps compare before and after shots taken from the same position and animate any portions that aren't an exact match.

No. 038: Detect Tampering of Personal Effects

CONOP: Utilize discreet alignments to determine tampering.

COA 1: Cardinal Bearings (Compass Alignment)

COA 2: Space and Depth (Thumb Measurement)

COA 3: Traps

Close door on "do not disturb" sign—if free-hanging upon return, assume the door was opened.

Use pocket lint and threads to set traps on drawers and doors.

DO NOT DISTURB

COA 4: Photo Trap Application (available on app store)

BLUF: Discreet alignment techniques should be non-alerting and easy to remember.

039 Determine Surveillance

Almost every criminal act, from purse snatching and other misdemeanors to sex crimes or acts of terrorism, involves some degree of preoperational surveillance. Though they may be focused on watching a target, criminals themselves are actually quite vulnerable to detection during this time—particularly if their targets (unlike the average civilian) remain alert and attuned to their surroundings.

To confirm surveillance, Violent Nomads search for "coincidences" repeated over time and distance, employing a multipronged approach governed by the acronym TEDD (Time, Environment, Distance, and Demeanor). But be subtle—it's advantageous to let criminals believe they've lost their target accidentally, rather than have them think the target is evading them.

Time: Is the same person or people observed repeatedly over time, in different environments? To determine whether this is the case, pay attention to the clock throughout the day.

Environment: Notice any people whose dress or body language does not fit the environment?

Distance: Are the same people popping up in environments separated by a fair amount of distance? For instance, was the same man in the dark glasses seen ten minutes ago in a neighborhood store (less suspicious) or two hours ago in a supermarket ten miles away (more suspicious)? Eliminate coincidence in order to confirm surveillance—test out theories by running errands across zip codes.

Demeanor: In a possible surveillance context, "demeanor" stands for both behavior and appearance. Be on the lookout for people whose dress or behavior does not fit the circumstances.

No. 039: Determine Surveillance

CONOP: Use TEDD to confirm surveillance or stalkers.

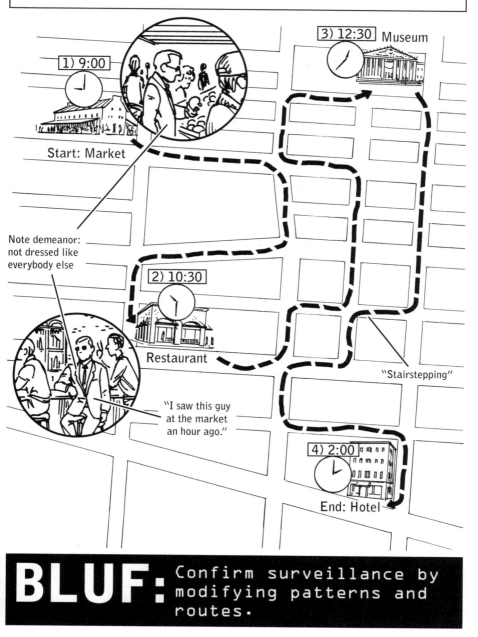

1) 9:00
Start: Market

Note demeanor: not dressed like everybody else

2) 10:30
Restaurant

"I saw this guy at the market an hour ago."

3) 12:30 Museum

"Stairstepping"

4) 2:00
End: Hotel

BLUF: Confirm surveillance by modifying patterns and routes.

040 Discreetly Lose Surveillance

The key to getting rid of a surveillance team without escalating a tail into a heated chase is letting them believe they have lost their target—and not the other way around. To lose a mobile surveillance team, forgo highly visible evasive driving techniques in favor of the following protocol:

Create an Accordion Effect: Break down a surveillance team by dragging it through an area with many lights and/or stop signs. A long stretch of stop-and-go traffic will thin out a team without alerting its members to the Nomad's agenda. The car closest to him may stay close, but the rest of the team will eventually get stuck several lights away. Unable to swap out with team members, the lone tail may grow wary of alerting his target and opt to disengage.

Stop and Start Frequently: Surveillance teams tend to lose targets on the start or stop of a movement—so increase the frequency of stops. An operative parked near an exit could take two right-hand turns out of the lot before the team realizes it's time to start moving.

Use Public Transportation: To lose a surveillance team by hopping on public transport, plan in advance. Arrive at a destination just as the bus or train is pulling up and hop on before the tail can mobilize.

Transit through Highly Populated Areas: Density and congestion make it difficult for a team to keep eyes on a target. When on foot, enter high-traffic spots such as malls, amusement parks, and tourist traps to increase the chance of a loss.

No. 040: Discreetly Lose Surveillance

CONOP: Make surveillance teams believe they lost the target through negligence, rather than by design.

COA 1: Create an accordion effect.

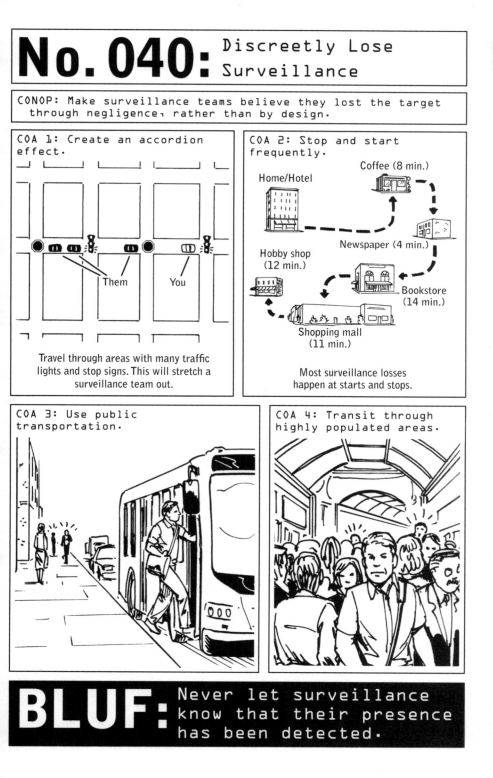

Them

You

Travel through areas with many traffic lights and stop signs. This will stretch a surveillance team out.

COA 2: Stop and start frequently.

Home/Hotel

Coffee (8 min.)

Newspaper (4 min.)

Hobby shop (12 min.)

Bookstore (14 min.)

Shopping mall (11 min.)

Most surveillance losses happen at starts and stops.

COA 3: Use public transportation.

COA 4: Transit through highly populated areas.

BLUF: Never let surveillance know that their presence has been detected.

041 Detect Tracking Devices

In these days of shrinking technology, affixing a magnetized tracking device to a vehicle is an all-too-easy proposition. Readily available for purposes from parenting to surveillance, tracking devices come in sizes as small as thumb drives—and they're also preinstalled in a variety of contexts, pinging the locations of mobile phones and rental cars alike. For operatives traveling internationally, it's safe to assume that any rental car will come pre-equipped with a built-in tracking device used to deter theft. But in the hands of an unfriendly host nation, there's no telling how this information could be used.

Communicating via satellite, cellular towers, and server banks, tracking devices can be either permanently mounted to a vehicle or temporarily magnetized to its frame. Because their signals cannot punch through metal, they cannot be hidden beneath the frame or metal parts of the car—which means there are specific places where they are usually found.

To avoid getting caught overtly inspecting a vehicle, listen for a telltale static. Turn off any cell phones, and set the radio to an AM station that's crackly and out of range. If an occasional ticking sound can be detected behind that fuzz, there is some kind of cellular device at work inside the car. (The sound arises from the interaction of the cellular signal with the radio's speaker wire and coil.)

Do not attempt to remove the tracking device if there is reason to believe that the tracking is nefarious rather than a matter of standard protocol; instead, come up with an excuse to trade in the car.

No. 041: Detect Tracking Devices

CONOP: Detect tracking devices through physical and/or technical inspection.

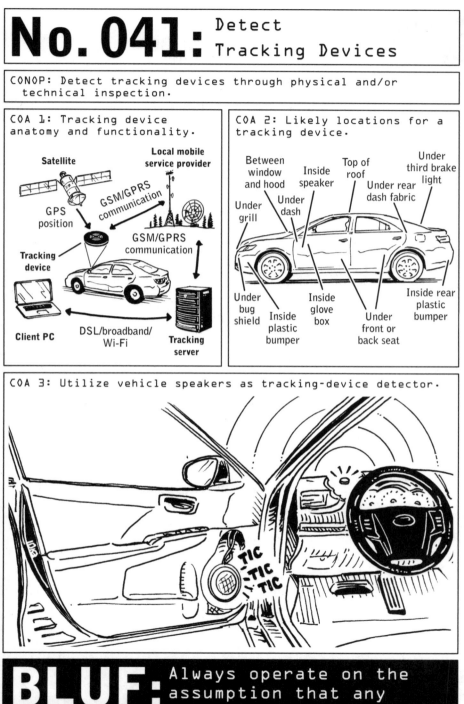

COA 1: Tracking device anatomy and functionality.

Satellite

Local mobile service provider

GPS position

GSM/GPRS communication

Tracking device

GSM/GPRS communication

Client PC

DSL/broadband/Wi-Fi

Tracking server

COA 2: Likely locations for a tracking device.

Between window and hood

Inside speaker

Top of roof

Under third brake light

Under rear dash fabric

Under grill

Under dash

Under bug shield

Inside plastic bumper

Inside glove box

Under front or back seat

Inside rear plastic bumper

COA 3: Utilize vehicle speakers as tracking-device detector.

TIC TIC TIC

BLUF: Always operate on the assumption that any movements may be tracked.

042 Deceive Surveillance Cameras

Capturing footage of our faces at traffic stops, ATM machines, and outside businesses from jewelry stores to pizza joints, surveillance cameras line the streets in major cities. And given how cheap they've become, they are now found in even remote parts of the world. To err on the safe side, a Violent Nomad always assumes he is being filmed and employs several methods of concealment and disruption to reduce the risk of being identified.

Disguise: Operatives avoid masks or outlandish disguises, Hollywood plot devices that will quickly get them spotted by third parties. Instead, they wear hats or head coverings.

Light: The auto-exposure feature on many cameras constricts the aperture in bright light—so shining a flashlight or LED directly into the camera will result in a lower-quality image, as will timing movements so that the sun is always behind an operative when he encounters a camera.

Static: A security camera's core signal travels down a copper conductor sheathed in layers of braided metal and rubber. Placing a steel razor blade in contact with that copper conductor will short the connection, temporarily disrupting the camera's video feed. After the blade slides through the rubber jacket, it is wiggled through the braided shield until it reaches the hard metal core. Left in place, the blade will cause the monitor to fill up with static. As soon as the razor is removed, the signal will return to normal.

No. 042: Deceive Surveillance Cameras

CONOP: Disrupt or prevent quality video capture.

COA 1: Light Disguise. Cover face with whatever the environment will allow.

COA 2: Bright Light. Infrared or visible light causes camera aperture to constrict.

COA 3: Video Feed Disruption. Razor slices into cable halfway and is left in place to bridge the shield and center conductor, causing static on monitors. Once razor is removed, monitor returns to normal.

Razor blade (halfway in)

Braided shield

Center conductor

Outer jacket

Foil shield

Dielectric

BLUF: Always assume surveillance cameras are watching.

PART V

ACCESS: CLANDESTINE BREAKING AND ENTERING

PICKING A LOCK

An operative typically prefers a method of clandestine entry that will allow him repeated access to the target's domicile or place of business, but mission timelines sometimes demand more immediate action. In such cases, the operative may revert to the time-honored practice of lock picking.

Though popular depictions of breaking and entering frequently show thieves bypassing locked doors with the cursory jiggle of a screwdriver, in reality it takes two hands and two tools to open a lock—one to lift the lock pins, and one to turn the cylinder.

Still, as the following pages will demonstrate, it is remarkably easy for intruders to bypass common door locks. The best prevention is a higher-quality door lock, but there are measures civilians can take to reinforce even the flimsiest of hotel room locks.

043 Create Improvised Lock-Picking Tools

While any lock with a key can theoretically be picked, high-security locks featuring pins that must be lifted *and* twisted probably won't be vulnerable to improvised instruments. Most pin tumbler and wafer locks, however, can be defeated with nothing more than a couple of paper clips and a significant amount of practice.

Using two paper clips, along with a pair of pliers and a flat file or hard surface, an operative can create improvised tools to simulate the actions of a rake pick and a tension wrench or torsion tool.

Larger, thicker-gauged paper clips are preferable, as they will hold up under pressure; bobby pins or the band metal used to hold shipping crates together can be used as an alternative.

Thinning the instruments will allow more room for maneuvering and ensure that both tools are able to fit inside the lock simultaneously. In the absence of a file, the floor or a wall can be used to sand them down.

No. 043: Create Improvised Lock-Picking Tools

CONOP: Construct lockpicks from paper clips.

COA 1: Following subsequent steps, use pliers to straighten paper clips into the shapes shown below. Straighten a clip in only one direction—rebending it will significantly weaken the metal.

Rake pick

Torsion tool

COA 2: Carefully form the ridges of the rake pick by bending the tip of the paper clip into a wave pattern.

COA 3: Loop the tail of the clip over and under to strengthen the handle.

COA 4: Carefully bend the tip of the second clip to form the torsion tool.

COA 5: Flatten the ends of both tools to make them easier to manipulate inside the lock.

COA 6: Be prepared for a time-intensive pursuit.

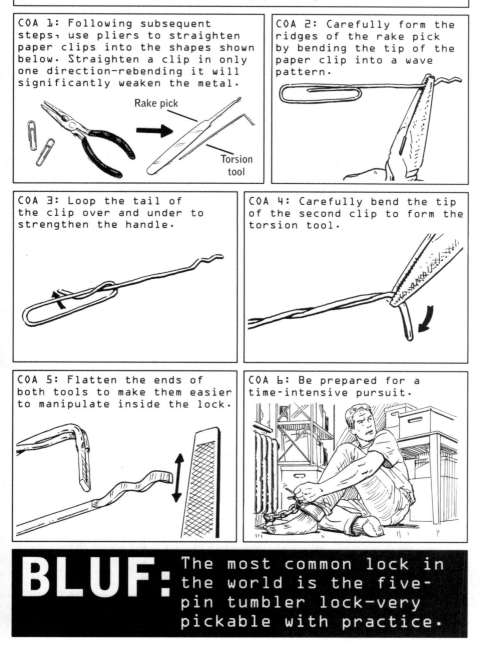

BLUF: The most common lock in the world is the five-pin tumbler lock—very pickable with practice.

044 Pick a Lock

A crosscut view of the interior of a common lock reveals its inner workings—along with its vulnerabilities. The lock case houses two rows of five pins, top and bottom, their lengths corresponding to the cuts on a key. (Known as a five-pin tumbler lock, this common model actually contains ten separate pins.)

When there's no key in the lock, springs in the top of the pin chamber push the top and bottom pins down so that they obstruct the lock's shear line. When a properly cut key is inserted into the lock, the pins are pushed up to the levels that clear the shear line. The cylinder is free to rotate, thereby retracting the deadbolt.

The trick to lock defeat is in simultaneously applying tension to the cylinder while moving the pins out of the way of the shear line; in the absence of a key, the rotational tension will hold them in place.

Using the nondominant hand, first insert the tension wrench or torsion tool and apply rotational pressure. Insert the pick tool with other hand, using it to move the pins, one by one, until they pop into unlocked position. Use the tip of the pick tool to find each pin, employing a rocking motion to lift it to the shear line.

With improvised or off-the-shelf lock-picking instruments on hand, a common pin tumbler lock can be defeated via a combination of patience, dexterity, and practice.

No. 044: Pick a Lock

CONOP: Open a lock by picking pins to shear line.

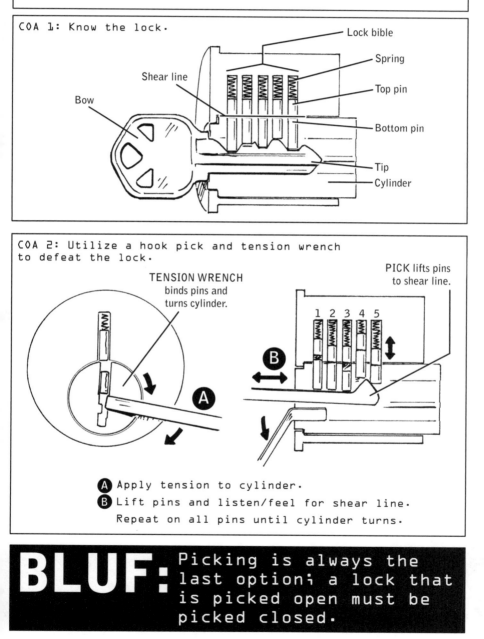

COA 1: Know the lock.

Lock bible

Spring

Top pin

Shear line

Bow

Bottom pin

Tip

Cylinder

COA 2: Utilize a hook pick and tension wrench to defeat the lock.

PICK lifts pins to shear line.

TENSION WRENCH binds pins and turns cylinder.

1 2 3 4 5

B

A

A Apply tension to cylinder.
B Lift pins and listen/feel for shear line.
Repeat on all pins until cylinder turns.

BLUF: Picking is always the last option; a lock that is picked open must be picked closed.

DUPLICATING A KEY

Because every lock that is picked open must be picked closed, lock picking is actually the option of last resort. Instead, whenever possible, operatives aim to temporarily appropriate and duplicate a target's key. Ensuring a method of repeated access to the target's home or business, this enables them to perform surveillance in small, undetectable increments over a period of days or weeks.

045 Clam a Key

Materials as ordinary and commonplace as a bar of soap, a patch of skin, or a piece of Styrofoam can be used to physically "clam" a key, producing an embossing that is the first step in duplication.

But when operatives are unable to make a physical impression of the target's key, a photograph provides one of the simplest and most effective means of replication. All that's needed as a window of opportunity is that split second in which the target momentarily places his keys on a restaurant table or bar counter.

Physical methods of clamming provide a more accurate embossing of the target's key but can be difficult to pull off. Access may present itself at any given moment, and the operative must be ready to act. In the absence of clamming tools, the operative can simply press the key against a soft patch of his own skin; the resulting mark will last several minutes. Once the operative has left the premises, tracing the outline with a marker or pen produces a rendering that will show up clearly in a photograph or photocopy. More-dependable results can be obtained by depressing keys into malleable surfaces such as bars of soap, Styrofoam cups or plates, or traditional key clams filled with modeling clay.

No. 045: Clam a Key

CONOP: Clam a target key to be duplicated later.

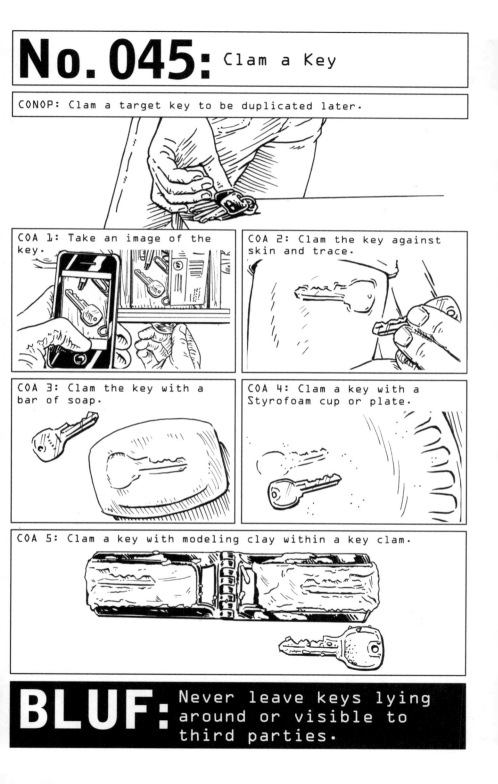

COA 1: Take an image of the key.

COA 2: Clam the key against skin and trace.

COA 3: Clam the key with a bar of soap.

COA 4: Clam a key with a Styrofoam cup or plate.

COA 5: Clam a key with modeling clay within a key clam.

BLUF: Never leave keys lying around or visible to third parties.

046 Clone a Key

Armed with nothing more than an aluminum soda can, a pen or pencil, a pair of scissors, and a paper clip, a Violent Nomad can effectively turn a key clamming into a duplicate key that will grant him direct access to the target's domicile or business.

A copy machine can render a true-to-size flat copy of the target key clamming. If working from a photograph, resize or photocopy prints to reflect actual key proportions.

Use scissors to carefully cut out a paper outline of the key. Set aside. Cut the top and bottom off of the aluminum can, then cut the remaining cylinder in half. Lay the key outline on top of the aluminum rectangle, then trace and cut out the key shape once more. This is the duplicate key—but because it is so malleable, a separate torsion tool is also needed.

To make one, straighten out a paper clip, then bend one end into an L shape.

Slide the aluminum key clone into the target lock, partially unlocking the mechanism by raising the lock pins to the shear line. The key clone will be too flimsy to turn, so insert the short end of the paper clip into the lock beneath it. Use the paper clip to turn the lock cylinder.

No. 046: Clone a Key

CONOP: Duplicate a target key via key cloning.

COA 1: Obtain clamming of target key (see #045) and highlight key embossing with Sharpie.

COA 2: Photocopy clamming in order to render a 1:1 ratio of target key.

COA 3: Cut out broad outline of photocopy of key. Trace paper key to aluminum cut from aluminum can. Cut out shape.

COA 4: Cut out key cuts from paper key; trace onto aluminum key blank and cut.

COA 5: Dispose of paper key. Aluminum key will lift target lock pins to proper combination, and paper clip will turn the cylinder and unlock the lock.

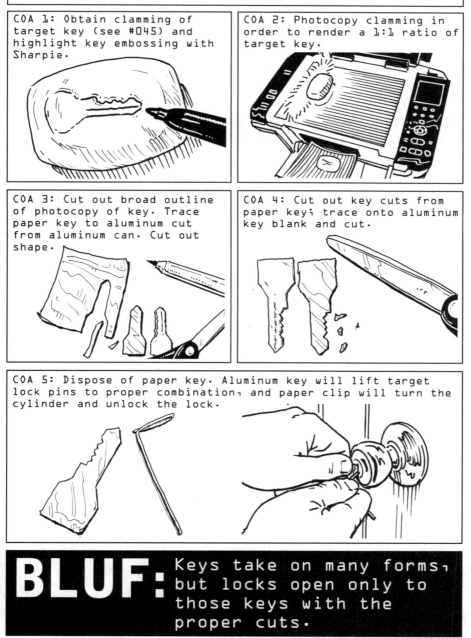

BLUF: Keys take on many forms, but locks open only to those keys with the proper cuts.

The central challenge in lock defeat is momentarily swiping the target's key in order to clone it (see page 114). In many instances, operatives cannot get close enough to a target to do so without compromising mission integrity and must thus proceed without a clone. If they seek one-time access to a target's residence, they may choose to pick the lock (page 110). But generally, once they negotiate access to a target's home or business, their goal is to provide themselves a repeatable, reliable means of reentry. Operatives want the ability to come and go without detection in order to accomplish the mission over several entries—a key can allow them to split an hour-long task into several five-, ten-, or fifteen-minute increments over a period of thirty days. They may also want to provide copies of the key to other government entities conducting compartmentalized operations.

In the absence of a clone, the key duplication technique of last resort is impressioning a lock. This time-intensive technique, one familiar to master locksmiths the world over, requires practice and many risky minutes spent at the target's door. But for anyone intent on gaining access to high-value documents and evidence, the time will be well spent.

To execute, use a primary trip to photograph the lock and determine what type of key blank to purchase. Or transit to the location with a set of reconnaissance key blanks purchased within the area of operation; these will have the greatest probability of providing a match.

With key blank, flat and round files, and pliers in hand, the painstaking process of manually impressioning the key begins. First, smooth down the key blank with the flat file. Insert the key blank into the lock, and jiggle it up and down. The lock pins will leave behind a row of telltale scratches—these become guidelines for key cuts. Using the round file, carefully file grooves at scratch points. Insert the key blank into the lock and repeat, filing it down at marked points until it finally clicks and turns.

No. 047: Impression a Lock

CONOP: Create a key to a lock by impressioning.

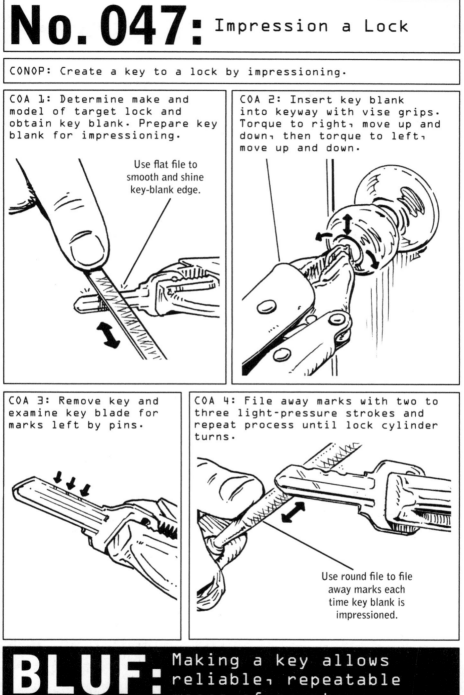

COA 1: Determine make and model of target lock and obtain key blank. Prepare key blank for impressioning.

Use flat file to smooth and shine key-blank edge.

COA 2: Insert key blank into keyway with vise grips. Torque to right, move up and down, then torque to left, move up and down.

COA 3: Remove key and examine key blade for marks left by pins.

COA 4: File away marks with two to three light-pressure strokes and repeat process until lock cylinder turns.

Use round file to file away marks each time key blank is impressioned.

BLUF: Making a key allows reliable, repeatable means of reentry.

048 Bypass a Hotel Room Door

Mandatory in many commercial buildings and hotels due to fire codes and disability laws, lever handle knobs allow a person crawling in a fire to reach up and quickly pull down on the knob to unlock the deadbolt. But beware: this accessibility feature also renders the locks vulnerable to intruders. When guests lock themselves out or lever handles malfunction, hotel staff members use an under-the-door lever lock tool to trip the lock from the hallway, and such a tool is easy to replicate using a hanger and piece of string. With a series of simple maneuvers, thieves and operatives can easily defeat this lock.

Construct an Under-the-Door Tool: Use a set of pliers to cut the hanger at two points, creating a small L-shaped hook and a larger J-shaped handle. Bend an additional "hook" into the L-shaped handle and tie a four-foot-long piece of string to this hook.

Breach the Door: Slide the L-shaped end of the tool under the target door, holding on to the free end of the string, and push it forward until the J-shaped end of the tool is about one inch away from the door.

Grasp the Doorknob: Roll the tool onto the curve of the J-shaped end until an audible tap on the other side of the door signals that the tool is now upright. Slide the tool toward the knob until it catches the lever handle.

Trip the Lock: Pull on the hanger and string to pull the handle down and disengage the lock.

Civilian BLUF: Lever handle knobs are easy to defeat, but additional protection may be obtained by obstructing the gap beneath the door with a towel (stuffed into the gap as securely as possible).

No. 048: Bypass a Hotel Room Door

CONOP: Unlock hotel room lever handles from a hallway.

COA 1: Construct an under-the-door tool utilizing a straightened hanger and string.

Adjust as necessary so that tool is a little longer than distance from door to lever handle.

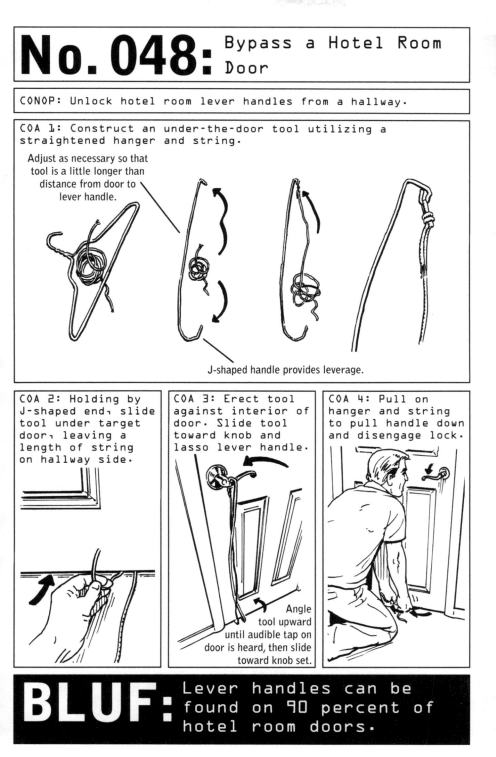

J-shaped handle provides leverage.

COA 2: Holding by J-shaped end, slide tool under target door, leaving a length of string on hallway side.

COA 3: Erect tool against interior of door. Slide tool toward knob and lasso lever handle.

Angle tool upward until audible tap on door is heard, then slide toward knob set.

COA 4: Pull on hanger and string to pull handle down and disengage lock.

BLUF: Lever handles can be found on 90 percent of hotel room doors.

049 Surreptitiously Unlatch Door Locks

Commonly found in both hotel rooms and homes, door chain and bar locks are the flimsiest of all locking mechanisms. But for operatives looking to access a target's room without leaving a trace, a forced entry that leaves behind a splintered doorframe and a broken lock is a method of last resort. Instead, operatives rely on a method of entry that sets the lock back into locked position upon departure.

A door that is secured by only a chain or bar lock will open about three inches—just enough space for an operative's or thief's forearm to squeeze through and create an auto-unlock device using a rubber band, a pushpin, and a length of dental floss.

On a chain lock, loop one end of the rubber band to the end of the chain, then stretch and pin the other end toward the center of the door. As the door closes, the increased tension on the rubber band will pull the chain out of the lock (see diagram).

On a bar lock, the technique is slightly more challenging. First, affix the rubber band to the bar using a "girth hitch" loop. Then, stretch the other end of the rubber band toward the doorframe (away from the center of the door) and pin it to the wall beside the door (see diagram).

To pull the lock closed as the door shuts, loop a double length of dental floss over one arm of the locking bar near its base; hold on to the ends of the floss while closing the door, then pull to lock. To retrieve the floss, pull it through the door opening by one end.

Civilian BLUF: Never rely on door chain or bar locks to secure doors. Always use your deadbolt.

No.049: Surreptitiously Unlatch Door Locks

CONOP: Breach locked door chain and bar locks.

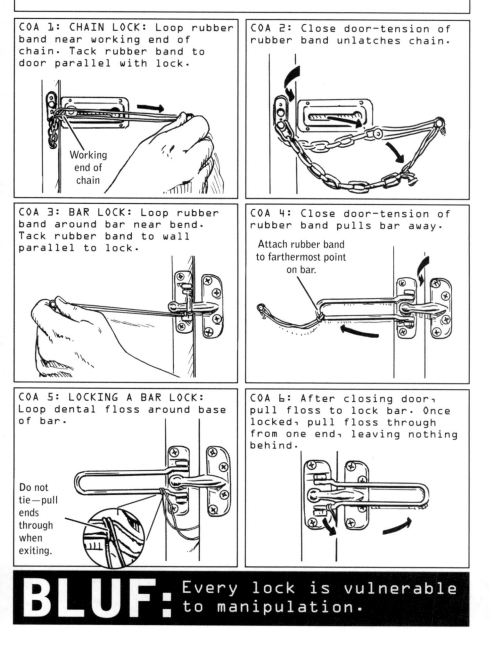

COA 1: CHAIN LOCK: Loop rubber band near working end of chain. Tack rubber band to door parallel with lock.

Working end of chain

COA 2: Close door-tension of rubber band unlatches chain.

COA 3: BAR LOCK: Loop rubber band around bar near bend. Tack rubber band to wall parallel to lock.

COA 4: Close door-tension of rubber band pulls bar away.

Attach rubber band to farthermost point on bar.

COA 5: LOCKING A BAR LOCK: Loop dental floss around base of bar.

Do not tie—pull ends through when exiting.

COA 6: After closing door, pull floss to lock bar. Once locked, pull floss through from one end, leaving nothing behind.

BLUF: Every lock is vulnerable to manipulation.

050 Defeat a Padlock

While padlocks have a heft that communicates a certain impenetrability, in reality they provide little more than a sense of false security to their owners. Operatives actually seek out entrances secured by padlocks, on the very assumption that they will be easy to defeat. Many are constructed quite flimsily, built with a loose tolerance that makes them extremely vulnerable to intruders. In some cases they can be bypassed entirely—the pieces to which the locks are affixed may themselves be vulnerable, as with hasps that can simply be unscrewed from a gate.

In order to defeat a padlock directly, a set of improvised shims can be made using a lightweight, pliable aluminum can and a pair of shears. Cutting out two rectangular pieces with semicircular tabs (see diagram) yields tools strong enough to take on most padlocks.

Slid down between the shackle and lock case, the shims are rotated so that their tongues move to the insides of the shackle and jostle the interior ball bearings aside. With the ball bearings pushed out of the indentation in the shackle, the padlock will unlock with upward pressure.

Civilian BLUF: When securing an entrance via padlock, be sure to select a top-of-the-line model and address any vulnerabilities in the surface to which the padlock will be mounted.

No. 050: Defeat a Padlock

CONOP: Create a padlock shim from an aluminum can.

COA 1: Obtain an aluminum can and hand shears.

COA 2: Cut the top and bottom off the can; then cut the cylinder in half to create a rectangular sheet. Draw two shim patterns onto the aluminum.

Patterns will vary in size, depending on the size of the shackle.

COA 3: Cut out tongued tabs as shown, folding their bases in half to allow more leverage in the lock.

Shim

1/2"

– FOLD –

3"

Shim grip

COA 4: To unlock shackle, slide shims down between shackle and lock case.

COA 5: Rotate shim handles to outside of shackles.

COA 6: Once both shims are in place, pull up on shackle to unlock.

BLUF: Most padlocks are knockoffs, making them vulnerable to shimming.

051 Covertly Access Locked Luggage

A locked suitcase presents no real impediment to a well-trained operative. Luggage locks can easily be opened with master keys or bypassed entirely by simply nudging the suitcase's zipper open with a ballpoint pen. But an operative conducting a search of a potential target's valuables always seeks to erase any trace of his actions. When attempting to retrieve valuable intelligence (or to plant eavesdropping technology or tracking devices that might render the target even more vulnerable), breaking into locked luggage without detection is key.

Because there's no telling whether a target has employed discrete alignment techniques (see page 94) in order to detect tampering, a Violent Nomad can never be too cautious. Together with the zipper breaking technique, the use of apps such as Photo Trap can help ensure that the target's belongings are left exactly as they were found.

Once the suitcase has been breached, off-the-shelf tracking devices can be inserted into its lining—the area between the wheels and the fabric often provides a discreet concealment area.

Civilian BLUF: Any object with a zipper closure can never truly be locked, and any suitcase made of cloth can ultimately be slashed open by a sharp instrument. For additional security, select hard-sided or trunk-style luggage with clamshell or clip closures.

No. 051: Covertly Access Locked Luggage

CONOP: Break into locked luggage without leaving a trace.

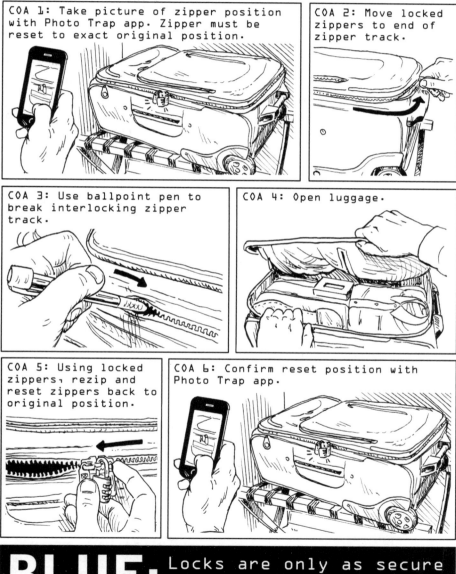

COA 1: Take picture of zipper position with Photo Trap app. Zipper must be reset to exact original position.

COA 2: Move locked zippers to end of zipper track.

COA 3: Use ballpoint pen to break interlocking zipper track.

COA 4: Open luggage.

COA 5: Using locked zippers, rezip and reset zippers back to original position.

COA 6: Confirm reset position with Photo Trap app.

BLUF: Locks are only as secure as the structure to which they are attached.

052 Open a Car Door with a Piece of String

Older-model cars with pull-up locks are vulnerable to the unlikeliest of break-in tools: a single piece of string, shimmied into the car through the opening between its window and frame. The most difficult part of the process is wedging the string past the rubberized weather seal around the top of the car doorframe. The older the car, the looser the seal will be.

Tie a Slipknot: Form a loop at the center of a six-foot-long piece of string or parachute cord. Cross one end of the string over and under the loop, creating a secondary loop. Hook the string back over and through the innermost loop, tightening it into a knot while maintaining the upper loop.

Shimmy the Knot into the Car: Working from the upper corner of the car door just above the lock, shimmy the knot and line into the car, keeping both ends of the string outside of the car. Pull back on the corner of the window to create an opening. In models where the glass windows don't have a frame around them, beware of exerting too much pressure on the window and causing the glass to shatter.

Snare the Thumb Puller: Guide the knot down toward the unlock mechanism and snare it with the loop.

Tighten the Knot: Pull both ends of the string in opposite directions to tighten the slipknot around the thumb puller.

Unlock the Door: Once the knot is tightened as much as possible, pull up on both ends of the string to unlock the door.

No. 052: Open a Car Door with a Piece of String

CONOP: Use a slipknot to unlock a vehicle door lock.

COA 1: Acquire six feet of string or parachute cord. Tie a slipknot at its center.

COA 2: Shimmy the knot and line into the car door.

COA 3: Snare the thumb puller.

COA 4: Pull string at opposing ends to tighten knot around thumb puller.

COA 5: Once looped, pull up and unlock door.

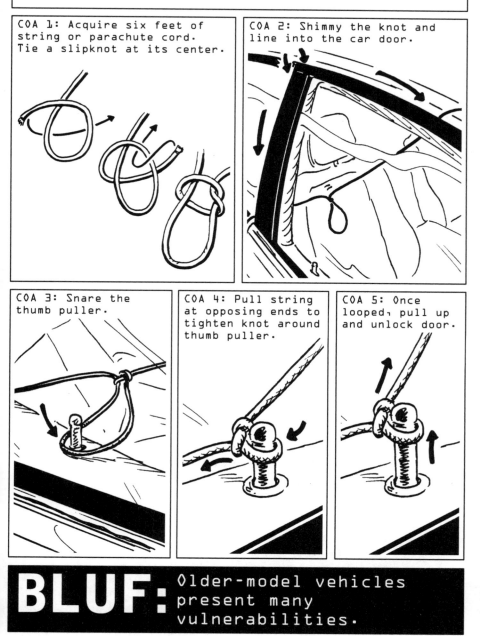

BLUF: Older-model vehicles present many vulnerabilities.

053 Discreetly Open Garage Doors

Lock picking can be an arduous and time-consuming task, which is why operatives tend to seek out workarounds such as clamming a target's key (page 114) or bypassing the lock altogether (page 120). In a home infiltration scenario, an attached garage with a door operated by an electric opening device provides a significant vulnerability for the Nomad to exploit.

Because they must slide up and back onto rail systems, garage doors are built with space along their top edges. By sliding a straightened-out hanger with a hook at its end between the garage door and the upper doorframe, the cable that disengages the automatic opening system can be hooked. Because most civilians use their automatic door closure systems as default locking mechanisms, this is all that is needed in order to "unlock" the door before manually opening it.

Once the operative has pulled the door open just a few feet, he will quickly slide beneath it and immediately pull the door closed. Entry to the house may now be possible—many homeowners fail to lock the door connecting the garage to the house. Even if that door is locked, there is now a safe and covered space from which to work on bypassing the lock for as long as necessary.

Civilian BLUF: Cut or tie off the manual-open cable of your garage door so that the cable becomes unreachable by a tool inserted at the top of the door. Even in a secured garage, never leave your car keys in your car. Lock the door between your house and garage to create layers of security.

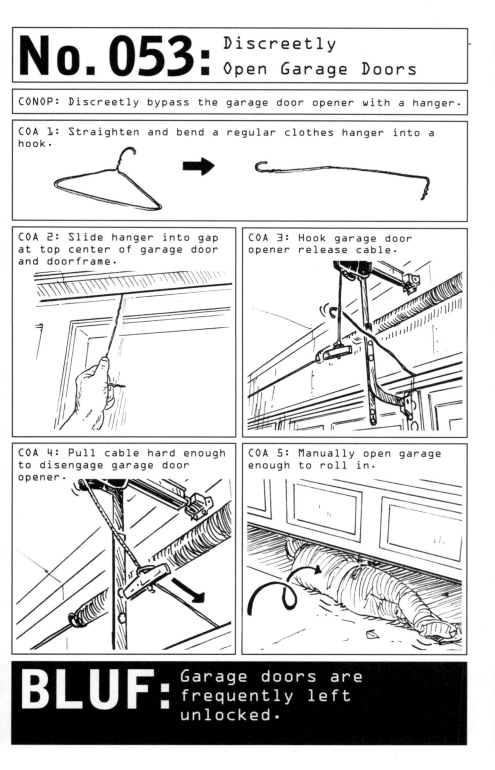

No. 053: Discreetly Open Garage Doors

CONOP: Discreetly bypass the garage door opener with a hanger.

COA 1: Straighten and bend a regular clothes hanger into a hook.

COA 2: Slide hanger into gap at top center of garage door and doorframe.

COA 3: Hook garage door opener release cable.

COA 4: Pull cable hard enough to disengage garage door opener.

COA 5: Manually open garage enough to roll in.

BLUF: Garage doors are frequently left unlocked.

PART VI

COLLECTION: AUDIO AND VIDEO INTELLIGENCE

054 Install an Audio Device

What is the optimal concealment spot for an audio surveillance mechanism? The answer depends on a compromise between available options, time spent on target, and achievable sound quality. While it is possible to create a functional listening device using little more than a mobile phone and a pair of headphones (see page 136), a botched installation will yield little in the way of actionable audio.

In selecting their install points, operatives attempt to determine where unguarded conversations are likeliest to occur (often in bedrooms or kitchens rather than living rooms) and aim for locations that put them at the "center of conversation."

Sound quality will also depend on the particularities of the concealment spot. In a car, a central console or dome light produces intelligible audio from both front- and backseat conversations, whereas a bug placed too near the front of the vehicle may pick up interference from the motor or stereo system. The molding of a television offers highly effective concealment but adds a plastic barrier that may interfere with sound quality.

Lastly, operatives will choose between a "hard install," a semi-permanent installation that utilizes parasitic power from a source such as a television or an electrical outlet, or a "soft install," which may be as simple as placing a recording device inside a box of tissues. The first option takes a great deal of time on target but means the operative never has to return in order to service the device. A soft installation may require dangerous return trips when the device runs out of batteries or maxes out its memory.

Civilian BLUF: While noise-canceling software can override the sounds of television or radio, it cannot process the sound of running water—which makes bathrooms in potentially compromised locations ideal spots for discreet conversations.

No. 054: Install an Audio Device

CONOP: Properly install audio devices in order to collect high-quality voice recordings.

COA 1: Install microphones at center of conversation.

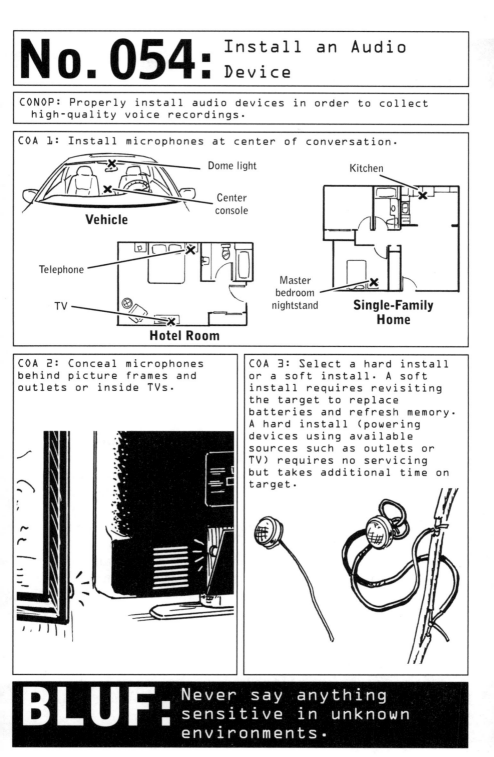

Dome light

Kitchen

Center console

Vehicle

Telephone

Master bedroom nightstand

Single-Family Home

TV

Hotel Room

COA 2: Conceal microphones behind picture frames and outlets or inside TVs.

COA 3: Select a hard install or a soft install. A soft install requires revisiting the target to replace batteries and refresh memory. A hard install (powering devices using available sources such as outlets or TV) requires no servicing but takes additional time on target.

BLUF: Never say anything sensitive in unknown environments.

055 Turn a Speaker into a Microphone

Stashing a voice-activated recording device in a target's room or vehicle is relatively simple, but without sound amplification, such a setup is unlikely to result in audible intelligence—a proper audio-surveillance system requires amplification via microphone. In the absence of dedicated tools, however, the Nomad can leverage a cell phone, an audio jack, and a pair of headphones into an effective listening device.

Because microphones and speakers are essentially the same instrument, any speaker—from the earbuds on a pair of headphones to the stereo system on a television—can be turned into a microphone in a matter of minutes. The simple difference between the two is that their functions are reversed. While a speaker turns electronic signals into sound, a mic turns sound into electronic signals to be manipulated and amplified.

The distinction turns on two wires, one positive (red) and one negative (black). Switching these wires reverses the polarity, and therefore the function, of the device (see diagram).

To execute, cut the outbound ends of the speaker wires and attach them to an audio jack. Plug the audio jack into the recording device.

Any small recording device can be employed, but using a phone set to silent and auto answer as a listening device has two advantages: It captures intelligence in real time and does so without the operative having to execute a potentially dangerous return trip on target to collect the device.

This audio installation technique is highly adaptable to a variety of environments. To set up vehicular surveillance, disable one of the car's rear speakers, plugging its wires into a voice recorder or phone; conceal the recording device in the dead space of a rear passenger door or a trunk's lining. In public places, earbuds dangling from a coat pocket can function as a discreet ambient surveillance station.

No. 055: Turn a Speaker into a Microphone

CONOP: Reverse the polarity of stereo speakers to turn them into microphones.

COA 1: Remove speaker housing. Locate positive and negative (red and black) wires. Rewire red wire to black terminal and black wire to red terminal.

COA 2: Cut and attach 2.5mm audio jack to opposing end of speaker wire.

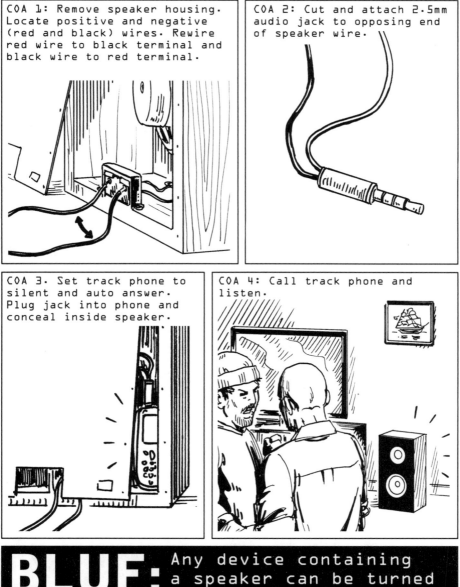

COA 3. Set track phone to silent and auto answer. Plug jack into phone and conceal inside speaker.

COA 4: Call track phone and listen.

BLUF: Any device containing a speaker can be turned into a microphone.

BUILDING AND CONCEALING A SURVEILLANCE CAMERA

For a Nomad, the optimal surveillance camera begins with an off-the-shelf product from a local superstore and ends with an object that blends into its environment to the point of invisibility. The starting point? A standard-issue baby monitor.

With cameras getting smaller and lighter by the day, it's possible to disguise a surveillance setup in a box of Kleenex, the casing of a gutted hardcover book, or the ample dead space in office equipment such as printers. But to secure a view over the exterior of a target's home or business in order to obtain positive identification on key holders and visitors, Nomads can use homemade plastic and disguise the camera as an innocuous rock or clump of dirt.

056 Construct and Install a Pinhole Camera

A pinhole camera starts with a visit to a superstore and the purchase of a wireless baby monitor. Once in hand, crack open the baby camera housing to reveal its contents (see diagram). Remove the components—a transmitter, a battery pack, and the camera lens—but keep them wired together. Discard the baby camera housing. Follow the instructions to create homemade plastic (see page 142), then place a toothpick in the eye of the camera lens and mold the plastic around the lens in the shape of a rock; the toothpick will create an indiscernible pinhole through which the camera will operate.

Paint the rock in a neutral color or a shade specific to the landscape outside the target's home and enclose the transmitter and battery pack in a waterproof ziplock bag or Tupperware container. Bury the container in a shallow hole (too deep and the transmitter's signal will fail) and set up the camera so that it captures people's faces as they enter and exit the building. To ensure that the camera's "look angle" is properly positioned, leave the toothpick in place until the last minute and use its angle to gauge the field of view.

For an additional layer of camouflage, apply spray glue to the rock during installation and cover it with dirt gathered on site. From a remote setup in a vehicle up to two hundred yards away, an operative will be able to observe the comings and goings on his monitor screen with limited risk of detection.

No. 056: Construct and Install a Pinhole Camera

CONOP: Construct a concealable video camera from a wireless baby monitor.

COA 1: Separate camera housing from camera, transmitter, and battery pack.

Baby camera casing
Monitor
Transmitter
Plastic
Battery pack
Lens
Toothpicks

COA 2: Conceal camera in plastic to look like a rock.

Place toothpick in lens; mold plastic around it.

Pinhole created for lens

COA 3: Paint rock neutral colors or colors specific to environment. Connect camera. Enclose transmitter and battery pack in waterproof housing or ziplock bag.

COA 4: Bury transmitter/battery pack in shallow hole, cover, and camouflage, with camera pointed in direction of target.

Camera

COA 5: Set up in vehicle to remotely observe bad guys.

BLUF: Wireless cameras are cheap, available, and easy to conceal.

All that is needed to conceal valuable data, keys, or surveillance devices such as cameras and microphones are two ingredients commonly found in any household kitchen: milk and vinegar. Heated and strained so that the milk's casein proteins coagulate into a rubbery, plasticlike substance, the mixture can be molded into any shape, drying to a claylike consistency.

In contrast to body cavity concealments focused on escape, or to mobile tech solutions focused on eliminating the Nomad's digital signature (page 194), plastic concealments are useful for camouflaging valuables or surveillance devices in a particular environment. The shape-shifting substance can be formed and painted to resemble rocks, bricks, logs, or any number of objects, making it a prime candidate for the dead drops Nomads use to surreptitiously communicate important data to associates.

Note: Heat time may vary depending on the microwave's power and settings.

Civilian BLUF: Cameras are everywhere—always assume you are being recorded.

No. 057: Make Homemade Plastic

CONOP: Make homemade plastic from milk and vinegar.

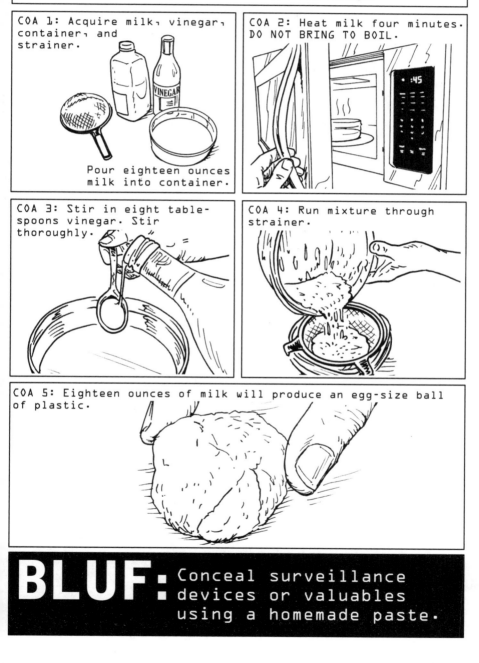

COA 1: Acquire milk, vinegar, container, and strainer.

Pour eighteen ounces milk into container.

COA 2: Heat milk four minutes. DO NOT BRING TO BOIL.

COA 3: Stir in eight table-spoons vinegar. Stir thoroughly.

COA 4: Run mixture through strainer.

COA 5: Eighteen ounces of milk will produce an egg-size ball of plastic.

BLUF: Conceal surveillance devices or valuables using a homemade paste.

058 Send Anonymous Emails

Password-protected email accounts and Wi-Fi connections are child's play to modern hackers, a class of information specialists that includes identity thieves, scam artists, and seasoned terrorists among its ranks. To thwart them, Nomads employ an anonymity network originally developed by members of the U.S. Naval Research Laboratory as a tool for secure communication. (Ironically, it has also become the favored network solution for criminals and black-market businesses of all stripes.)

Tor, the name of the network, prevents forensic traceback by encrypting and bouncing information through a chain of volunteer servers all over the world. By disguising the sender's point of origin, the network protects Nomads from third parties attempting to find out their geolocation; an anonymous email account with no connection to the Nomad's name or identity provides an additional layer of security.

Though free Wi-Fi hotspots are known for their lack of security and vulnerability to hackers, they can be useful to a Nomad who's wary of having his home or hotel connection tapped. To set up an anonymous browsing session, transit to a location that falls outside regular patterns, then access a free Wi-Fi connection that does not require a login or password. Download Tails, a user-friendly operating system that uses Tor as its backdrop and saves no browsing information. Once loaded, use Tails to create a new, completely anonymous email address. Follow the example of citizens in authoritarian regimes who, wishing to further decrease the span of their digital footprints, will often share email accounts with close associates. Instead of sending and receiving emails, they keep their communications secure by responding back and forth on draft emails, thereby never creating any potentially alerting traffic.

No. 058: Send Anonymous Emails

CONOP: Communicate anonymously via email, leaving zero forensic traceback.

COA 1: Transit to a public location not associated with home or work. Access a free Wi-Fi hotspot in a neighborhood shopping center or café.

COA 2: Download the app Tails.

COA 3: Using Tails as Internet browser, create new email address.

BLUF: Never trust the Internet—even the most secure networks have loopholes.

059 Hide Information in Plain Sight

No matter how carefully a Nomad covers his tracks, any exchange of digital information presents the possibility of a security breach. So operatives secure their messages with a multipronged system, layering various forms of encryption into communications sent through an anonymity network and via false email addresses (page 144). Just as spies once concealed information-filled microdots on the head of a pin, today operatives embed text documents into digital images that must be decompressed to reveal their contents.

To create a rudimentary form of encryption, start with a program such as TextEdit or Notepad. Avoid any word processing software that is connected to an update mechanism; documents created in such a program may be recoverable by third parties, even if they aren't being saved to a hard drive or to the cloud.

Before composing a message, paste an innocuous image into the text document.

Type sensitive information above or below the image. Change the font color to white and/or the font to a symbol for additional cover. In the short term, this will conceal activities from onlookers while the message is created. When the message is sent, the image file size will serve as a front, disguising any additional space taken up by the text.

No. 059: Hide Information in Plain Sight

CONOP: Conceal sensitive information within an innocent picture.

COA 1: Open TextEdit or Notepad in a secure location with screen pointed out of view. If possible, sit with back against wall.

COA 2: Cut/paste an innocent image into TextEdit or Notepad document.

COA 3: Type sensitive information above or below image.

BLUF: Image files will readily conceal additional text.

060 Hide and Extract Data Using Everyday Photos

When a suspicion of surveillance is confirmed, there is no such thing as a surfeit of caution. The Nomad hunkers down, limiting anything but the most essential communications and meeting associates in crowded public places. If he must send out information, a single form of encryption or covert messaging does not suffice—varying his methodologies will make it more difficult for potential code breakers to determine pattern and unlock his code.

Although elaborate, a method of encryption that relies on staging a physical artifact within a photograph deceives the human eye while foiling any kind of automated decryption software.

To set up the decoy, acquire a high-megapixel digital camera. (A smartphone camera will not produce images of high-enough quality.) Handwrite or print the message on paper. Conceal the physical artifact in the background of a posed shot—at the base of a building or camouflaged on a busy bulletin board in the background of a group shot.

Photograph the scene with the entire image in focus, then zoom in on the resulting image to make sure the message is legible.

In storing or emailing the image, be sure to save it at full resolution. Merge the image into a set of innocuous photographs. Downloaded to a flash drive and smuggled into a dead drop, or attached to a draft email on an account shared with associates (see page 144), the set will reveal its true contents only to those who know to search for them.

No. 060: Hide and Extract Data Using Everyday Photos

CONOP: Conceal sensitive information in an image's background.

COA 1: Acquire high-megapixel camera.

COA 2: Place sensitive information within background of posed shot.

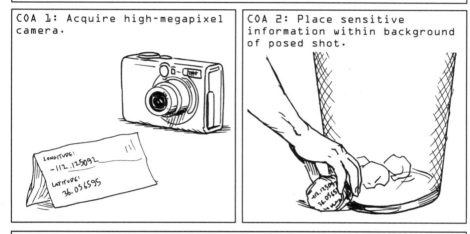

COA 3: Take photograph with entire image in focus. Email image to intended recipients and delete image from camera.

BLUF: The best encryption methods foil both software and the human eye.

PART VII

OPERATIONAL ACTIONS: DENY, DISRUPT, DISABLE

061 Draw a Concealed Pistol

Many gun-carrying civilians mistakenly practice their target shooting to the exclusion of related competencies. One frequently neglected area, the art of rapidly and seamlessly drawing a concealed weapon, is crucial to successful self-defense. When confronting an assailant who already has his weapon in play, a delay of even a half second or less will seriously compromise chances of survival—so operatives know that working on drawing technique (always with an unloaded weapon) and understanding the intricacies of each particular holster are crucial. Two frequent problems are fumbling the draw and drawing the holster along with the weapon.

Drawing a Weapon under an Untucked Shirt: A draw occurs in a single seamless motion that can be broken down into three distinct phases. In the first, the operative uses his thumb to "hook and sweep" his shirt out of the way, efficiently moving the fabric aside to prevent the weapon from getting tangled up in its folds. In the second, his nondominant hand holds up his shirt while his drawing hand lifts the weapon out of the holster. In the third, his nondominant hand becomes the support hand as he pops the wrist of his drawing hand and points the weapon toward the target. All the while, his eyes remain fixed on the target.

Drawing a Weapon under a Coat: A coat that swings forward while the operative attempts to draw can be a very real liability— one that's neutralized by the simple trick of weighting down the jacket with a roll of coins. Use the drawing hand to brush the jacket back while simultaneously drawing the weapon.

In both cases, the crucial support hand helps stabilize aim while quickening the draw—the human body functions more rapidly and efficiently when both sides are performing parallel actions in tandem.

No. 061: Draw a Concealed Pistol

CONOP: Avoid common pitfalls when drawing a concealed pistol.

COA 1: Draw from beneath an untucked shirt.

 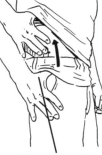  

| Prepare to "hook and sweep." | Thumb hooks shirt. Fingers sweep for pistol. Eyes on target. | Non-draw hand supports draw hand to clear shirt. | Once clear of holster, pop wrist and point weapon toward target. |

COA 2: Draw from beneath a coat.

| Place roll of coins in draw-side pocket. | Coins provide weight to keep jacket back while drawing weapon. | Once pistol is clear of holster, pop wrist and point weapon toward target. | Secondary hand supports drawing hand to clear weapon faster and aid in weapon retention. |

BLUF: Winning a gunfight starts with the draw.

For drivers and passengers caught in enemy crossfire, the first line of defense against armed attackers should be a rapid getaway by car. If driving away isn't possible, running for cover outside the vehicle is preferable to hunkering down. When bullets are flying, a stationary vehicle can quickly become a glass-enclosed coffin.

But for skilled operatives confined in their vehicle, a quick draw and an understanding of the dynamics of shooting through glass may mean the difference between life and death.

The question of where to holster a weapon for ease of access while driving depends on the individual driver, but for a right-handed person, a weapon holstered on the left hip will be accessible via a cross-draw but unimpeded by the seat-belt buckle.

When taking aim, leaning back and down affords cranial protection and keeps the shooter out of view and away from glass. Windshields are convex, curved surfaces whose arc tends to alter the bullet's pathway. To correct, operatives aim low; a shot aimed through a windshield at the target's pelvis should hit at chest level.

Operatives always fire multiple rounds, the first to break glass and the second to hit the target, bracing for a jolt. Because the first shot is fired in a confined environment, the resulting noise and pressure will be acute.

Most car windows are tempered and laminated so that they will break into petals that stick together rather than flying apart into shards. But when dealing with glass of any kind, serious injury can occur. If possible, push or kick the spidered glass out of the way for safety and improved aim.

No. 062: Shoot from a Vehicle

CONOP: Safely and accurately shoot from a vehicle and through glass.

COA 1: Practice drawing weapon with and without seat belt on.

COA 2: Lean back, away from target and glass-out of view of bad guys and a safe distance from window once glass starts flying.

COA 3: Aim low when shooting through windshield; curve of windshield will cause bullet to hit target high.

COA 4: Always fire multiple rounds: the first to break glass and the second to hit target.

BLUF: Always dismount vehicle when possible; if trapped, fire as many rounds as possible.

063 Win a Knife Fight

Easy to acquire and menacing to behold, knives are often used by common criminals who value their intimidation factor but lack a basic knowledge of knife fighting. For this reason, operatives know that learning proper knife-fighting techniques can play a critical factor in surviving an attack.

Guarding the Weapon: Protect vital organs from an opponent's knife and prevent the knife from being snatched by holding up a sacrificial guard hand and rotating the torso sideways. Turn knuckles toward the attacker to protect the arteries and veins on the inner wrist and forearm.

Knife Grip: An operative always maintains a full grip on his knife handle. Leaving the thumb stretched out over the top of the handle is extremely unsafe, so he curls his thumb around the handle to prevent injury and prohibit an opponent from taking the knife away.

Angles of Attack: To weaken an opponent, stab and slice along one of the eight angles of attack. This kind of motion enables the operative to filet a muscle apart, disabling the opponent and allowing the operative to gain the upper hand.

Cut Points: In a life-or-death struggle, an operative will try to stab an opponent in one of the body's large arteries to cause a lethal injury. The femoral artery, located on the inside of each thigh, has the greatest chance of being left unguarded.

Civilian BLUF: A knife that is not used safely provides no defense at all—it's more likely to imperil the user than to wound his attacker.

No. 063: Win a Knife Fight

CONOP: Use a knife as a targeted and effective weapon of self-defense.

COA 1: Guarding the Weapon

COA 2: Proper Knife Grip

COA 3: Angles of Attack

1
7   3
6   5
4   8
2

COA 4: Cut Points

Subclavical   Carotid

Aorta

Brachial

Radial

Femoral

BLUF: Knives are everywhere; know how to use one when crisis strikes.

When operatives shoot, they aim to kill—and when they strike, they aim for a knockout.

The key to achieving a knockout punch is to land the hit in such a way that it will cause the brain to bounce back and forth in the cerebrospinal fluid. A hard punch that lands on the temple, jaw, or chin can create injuries in both the front of the brain (a "coup" injury) and the back of the brain (a "contrecoup" injury), causing the opponent to lose consciousness and giving the operative plenty of time to escape.

The power in a well-executed punch comes from a rotational action in the core, amplified by the momentum of a double step forward. To make sure the punch lands forcefully, an operative will aim his knuckles through the back of the skull. Before throwing the punch, he'll employ a series of jabs with his nondominant hand to distract and wear down the opponent, using the element of surprise to deliver a hard-hitting straight punch with his dominant hand.

While hand-to-hand combat is never strategically desirable, even the best-laid plans are subject to unexpected developments. Whether caught off guard while picking a lock or simply a victim of being in the wrong place at the wrong time, the operative may face any number of opponents who are incidental to his mission. Drawing a weapon in such a scenario would attract too much notice, so when taken by surprise the operative seeks to knock out his opponent and clear the premises as quickly as possible.

No. 064: Strike for a Knockout

CONOP: Deliver a fight-ending right cross.

COA 1: Points of Impact for Increased Odds of a Knockout

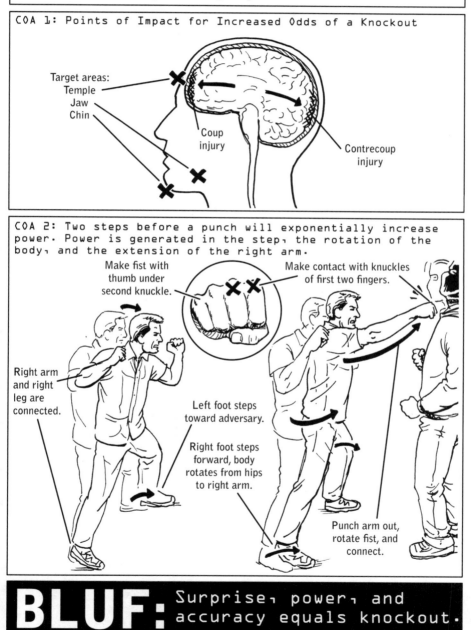

Target areas:
Temple
Jaw
Chin

Coup injury

Contrecoup injury

COA 2: Two steps before a punch will exponentially increase power. Power is generated in the step, the rotation of the body, and the extension of the right arm.

Make fist with thumb under second knuckle.

Make contact with knuckles of first two fingers.

Right arm and right leg are connected.

Left foot steps toward adversary.

Right foot steps forward, body rotates from hips to right arm.

Punch arm out, rotate fist, and connect.

BLUF: Surprise, power, and accuracy equals knockout.

065 Deliver a Devastating Elbow Strike

Trained to execute deadly assaults under any possible circumstance, Violent Nomads are well versed in the many forms of hand-to-hand combat—and they are always looking for the most efficient way to end a fight.

The elbow is the hardest and sharpest point on the human body. When combined with momentum and a calculated angle of attack, an elbow strike can result in a knockout, breaking skin and causing serious injury. Though both punching and kicking can potentially knock out an opponent, elbow strikes offer more maneuverability when engaging combatants in close proximity—and unlike punches, they can be employed in the all-too-common event that fights are taken to the ground.

Proper body positioning begins with a bent elbow, with the active hand open and the thumb anchored to the chest. Keeping the thumb anchored to the chest prevents the arm from straightening while striking. The power in an elbow strike comes largely from the rotation of the core, with the elbow becoming the temporary holding spot for that momentum. Straightening the arm dilutes momentum and increases recovery time.

The ulna, a bladelike bone that runs through the forearm, can be recruited as a secondary point of contact; keeping the hand open prevents the forearm muscles from constricting and enveloping the ulna, allowing the sharp and deadly bone to reveal itself.

The takeaway? Aiming an elbow at the throat, temple, or chin will result in a strike with a good chance of stunning or seriously debilitating an opponent.

No. 065: Deliver a Devastating Elbow Strike

CONOP: Cut and crush an adversary's head with proper elbow strikes.

COA 1: Elbow Strike Anatomy and Physiology

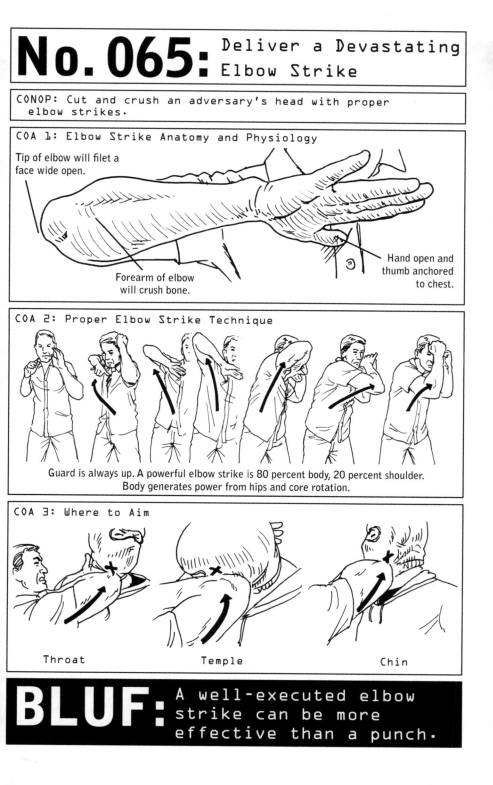

Tip of elbow will filet a face wide open.

Forearm of elbow will crush bone.

Hand open and thumb anchored to chest.

COA 2: Proper Elbow Strike Technique

Guard is always up. A powerful elbow strike is 80 percent body, 20 percent shoulder. Body generates power from hips and core rotation.

COA 3: Where to Aim

Throat

Temple

Chin

BLUF: A well-executed elbow strike can be more effective than a punch.

066 Make an Improvised Taser

Nothing could be less alerting than the sight of a tourist taking photographs—and that's good news for Nomads looking to create improvised self-defense weapons out of ordinary disposable cameras.

Nonlethal options for self-defense are crucial for average citizens and operatives alike, and the use of Tasers is legal across most of the United States. Off-the-shelf models, however, aren't always easy to come by, so Nomads must sometimes resort to an improvised hack by purchasing a disposable camera within the area of operation.

Following a series of modifications, the camera becomes a highly effective Taser—rewired so that the electricity normally used to power its flash is directed into two protruding screws, their charge powerful enough to temporarily incapacitate an assailant. An opponent hit with such a charge is likely to fall to the ground and be incapacitated for several minutes. A charge of anywhere from 120 to 380 volts will radiate through tissue and nerves, interfering with the brain's communication with muscles by creating static within the body. The result—impaired motor skills and involuntary muscle contractions—creates a powerful, nonlethal option for self-defense. To construct, trained operatives carefully follow these steps:

Drain the Capacitor: Before taking the camera apart, it is absolutely essential to remove the battery and depress the flash button. This will drain the capacitor of any stored electricity and prevent an accidental shock during assembly. If the capacitor is not properly drained, the risk of injury is very high.

Take the Camera Apart: Carefully remove the camera housing, then remove the circuit board, flash, film, and battery. Break apart the flashbulb assembly and the circuit board.

Prep the Tools: Acquire a screwdriver, a pair of wire strippers, two four-inch lengths of insulated wire, and two small screws. Before discarding the roll of film, cut and reserve a small piece.

Rewire the Camera: Strip the lengths of electrical wire at both ends. Wrap the wire ends around the heads of the screws. Twist the screws into the camera housing in the space where the film roll once sat. Wrap the opposing wire ends to the capacitor posts and tape to secure. This redirects the camera's charge from its battery into the two screws.

Put the Camera Back Together: Mount the circuit board into its original location, tucking in the electrical wire alongside it.

Insert the Safety Mechanism: Place the piece of reserved film between the battery and the battery terminal post to prevent the mechanism from accidentally discharging.

Replace the Housing: With its exterior cardboard casing replaced, the camera will look virtually indistinguishable from the models found in the backpack of any typical tourist.

Incapacitate the Opponent: To use the improvised Taser, employ a stabbing motion to drive the screws into the opponent's flesh. A touch will deliver a significant jolt, but in the event that the device doesn't discharge, breaking the skin should injure an attacker enough for the operative to gain the upper hand and make a rapid escape.

Note: Creating an improvised Taser is much more dangerous than it seems. Anyone attempting to do so should avoid touching the camera's capacitor or any part of its circuit board while the capacitor is charged. The electricity will discharge, causing a significant and potentially disabling shock. Only discharge the Taser in cases of extreme emergency.

No. 066: Make an Improvised Taser

CONOP: Modify a disposable flash camera into a Taser.

COA 1: Acquire a disposable camera with flash. Remove battery and press flash button—this will drain capacitor of any stored electricity.

COA 2: Carefully break apart camera housing and remove all parts: the plastic camera housing, circuit board, and flash and battery. Break away flashbulb assembly from circuit board.

COA 3: Acquire screwdriver, electrical tape, two four-inch lengths of insulated wire, two small screws, and a piece of film from camera.

COA 4: Strip both ends of four-inch wires. Wrap wire ends near screw heads.

COA 5: Twist screws into front housing where film roll once sat.

COA 6: Wrap opposing wire ends to capacitor posts and tape as needed.

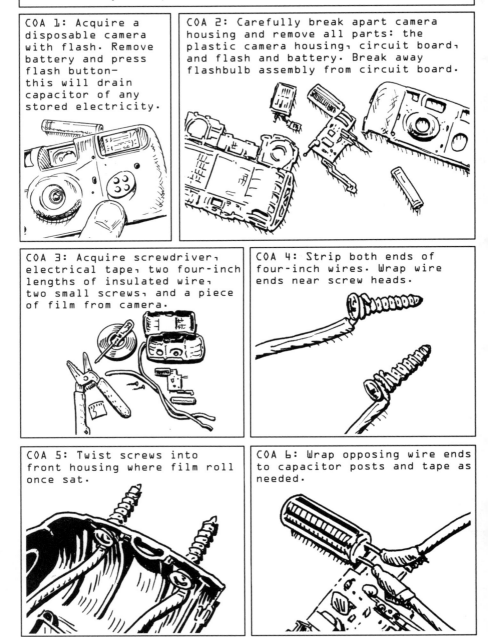

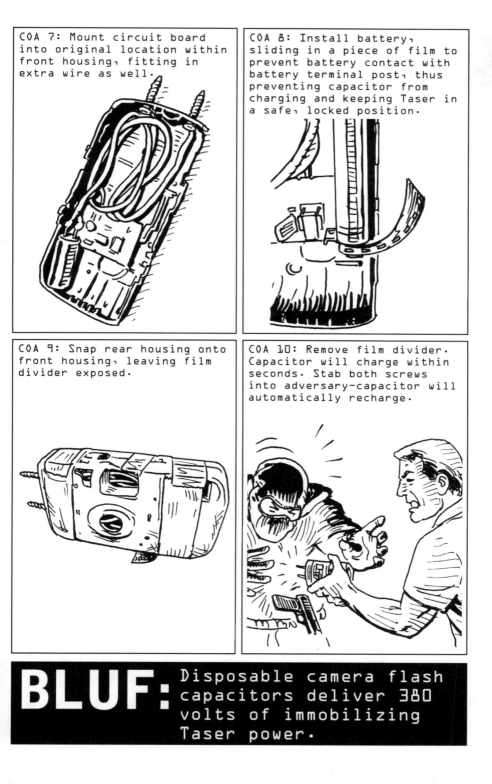

COA 7: Mount circuit board into original location within front housing, fitting in extra wire as well.

COA 8: Install battery, sliding in a piece of film to prevent battery contact with battery terminal post, thus preventing capacitor from charging and keeping Taser in a safe, locked position.

COA 9: Snap rear housing onto front housing, leaving film divider exposed.

COA 10: Remove film divider. Capacitor will charge within seconds. Stab both screws into adversary—capacitor will automatically recharge.

BLUF: Disposable camera flash capacitors deliver 380 volts of immobilizing Taser power.

067 Make an Improvised Explosive Device

In the absence of backup from fellow teammates, the operative looking to infiltrate a target's home must rely on improvised diversionary devices to distract the enemy's security unit. Used as part of military campaigns for centuries, diversions are particularly helpful for combatants working alone.

Two diversionary devices can be made from a disposable lighter. The first creates a momentary flash that will temporarily blind an opponent without damaging surrounding property (see page 168); the second launches an explosion equivalent to that created by a quarter stick of dynamite. Unlike Molotov cocktails and many other types of homemade explosive devices, this tool can be set off without advance modifications—which means it won't arouse suspicion if the operative is searched. All that's needed is tape and a lighter.

To create an explosion sizable enough to cause injury, damage property, and create a sustained sense of disorder, operatives choose a model fueled by compressed rather than liquid gas; though no longer sold in the United States due to their associated hazards, compressed gas lighters can readily be found overseas.

The trick works by loosening the flame adjustment gear from the lighter body until gas begins to leak. When the striker wheel is rolled to light the flame and the lighter is mounted at a downward angle with tape or zip ties, the flame will begin to melt the plastic casing. After a minute or two, the flame will burn through the casing, igniting all the gas in the canister in one fell swoop.

No. 067: Make an Improvised Explosive Device

CONOP: Construct an improvised diversionary explosive device.

COA 1: Acquire tape and lighter with adjustable flame. Remove flame guard.

Flame guard

COA 2: Slide ratchet to the + position to increase flame height.

COA 3: Lift ratchet to disconnect from flame adjustment gear. From the lifted position, move ratchet back to - position. Push down and slide to + position again.

COA 4: Continue to repeat process until lighter leaks gas on its own.

COA 5: Tape or zip-tie to target at angle, with ratchet facing down.

COA 6: Lighter will melt its own casing, then ... BOOM.

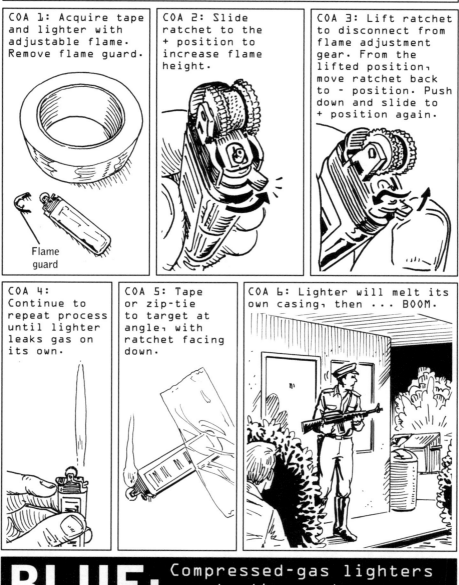

BLUF: Compressed-gas lighters create the most effective diversions.

068 Make a Diversionary "Flash" Device

Explosions, car accidents, fire alarms, power outages . . . These are just some of the "incidents" that seem to follow operatives around the globe—handy diversions that draw the attention of law enforcement officials, bystanders, or targets while the Nomad accomplishes his mission and vanishes into the night. In the face of sudden attack, diversions can also be used to facilitate escape, which is why carrying a discreet and portable diversionary device can be a lifesaver. Made in two minutes or less from an ordinary disposable lighter, the improvised device creates a blinding flash that, when used in darkness, can impair the human eye for up to ten minutes.

Mimicking the action of a stun grenade or "flash bang" device, the device works by isolating and heating up the lighter's flint— made of metal compounds that heat up quickly and produce a burst of incandescence upon combustion. When the heated flint hits the ground, the resulting flash is significant enough to be mistaken for an explosion. In essence, the gesture takes the lighter's lifetime of spark and uses it up all at once.

No. 068: Make a Diversionary "Flash" Device

CONOP: Use lighter parts to create a temporary blinding flash of light.

COA 1: Remove flame shroud.

COA 2: Remove striker wheel, flint, and flint spring.

Striker wheel

Flint

Flint spring

COA 3: Twist flint spring around flint.

COA 4: Heat flint until red hot (thirty seconds to one minute).

COA 5: Throw flint at ground to create one brilliant spark.

BLUF: A flash of light in total darkness can impair the human eye for up to ten minutes.

069 Make a Molotov Cocktail

The classic weapon of rebellion and urban warfare, the Molotov cocktail earned its moniker during World War II and has been around since the Spanish Civil War. To this day, the incendiary device remains the weapon of choice for disenfranchised agitators and anyone who lacks access to more sophisticated tools of combat. Because it can be launched over barricades or gates, it creates an option for street-level combat targeting highly guarded buildings or compounds.

For Violent Nomads seeking to disguise their actions as those of ordinary citizens, a Molotov cocktail provides a quick-to-assemble solution that can be thrown from a distance and sow a vast amount of chaos—without leaving any trace of governmental involvement. Apart from its obvious offensive uses, it may be employed as part of a campaign of psychological warfare (page 186) or as a diversionary tactic, drawing the attention of onlookers and security forces to a flaming car while the Nomad stealthily infiltrates a target building.

Though a basic version can be made by funneling fuel into a glass bottle, additions of motor oil and soap create a more flammable device. Motor oil, being thicker than gasoline, creates a longer-lasting fire. Shavings of soap create a gelling effect (particularly if the mixture is left to sit overnight), making for a potent napalmlike substance that spreads and sticks to surfaces as it burns. A fuel-soaked tampon becomes a flammable stopper and fuse. When the fuse is lit and the bottle thrown, the glass shatters upon impact, igniting a deadly and fast-moving fire.

No. 069: Make a Molotov Cocktail

CONOP: Construct and deliver diversionary Molotov cocktails.

COA 1: Acquire fuel, oil, bar of soap, tampon, glass bottle, and matches.

COA 2: Mix five cups fuel, one cup oil, and the shavings of half a bar of soap. (Soap will "gel" the mixture into napalm.)

COA 3: Plug bottle with fuel-soaked tampon.

COA 4: Light tampon fuse and launch.

BLUF: Molotov cocktails can be used to create a vast amount of chaos.

070 PIT a Target Vehicle

Most drivers tend to feel relatively safe when they're inside their vehicles. Especially when traveling through familiar areas, they become complacent, failing to pay attention to their surroundings—which is why targeting a bad guy's vehicle along the most vulnerable part of his route provides a solid option for Nomads looking to create an "accident."

As experts in both offensive and defensive driving techniques, Violent Nomads know how to turn an automobile into a highly effective weapon. A properly executed vehicular attack will incapacitate or eliminate a target without any attribution to official channels. One such method is the PIT (Precision Immobilization Technique). Used for decades by U.S. law enforcement, PITing is a pursuit tactic that forces a fleeing car to abruptly spin sideways, causing the driver to lose control and come to a stop.

The key to PIT maneuvers is for the operative to maintain his speed throughout the collision process. PITing at speeds of less than thirty-five miles per hour will cause the targeted vehicle to spin sideways and crash. PITing at any speed greater than thirty-five miles per hour is considered a lethal technique that will likely result in the targeted vehicle rolling over completely; high-center-of-gravity vehicles such as SUVs and vans are susceptible to rolling over if PITed at speeds of less than thirty-five miles per hour.

The highly skilled Nomad will conduct a PIT maneuver where there is the least likelihood of being observed, seamlessly speeding away from the scene and any potential witnesses.

No. 070: PIT a Target Vehicle

CONOP: Disable a target vehicle using the Precision Immobilization Technique.

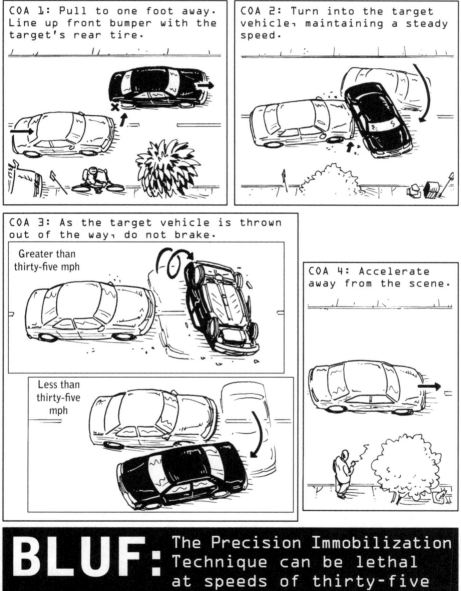

COA 1: Pull to one foot away. Line up front bumper with the target's rear tire.

COA 2: Turn into the target vehicle, maintaining a steady speed.

COA 3: As the target vehicle is thrown out of the way, do not brake.

Greater than thirty-five mph

Less than thirty-five mph

COA 4: Accelerate away from the scene.

BLUF: The Precision Immobilization Technique can be lethal at speeds of thirty-five miles per hour or greater.

071 Pistol Disarmament: Pointed at Chest

If a masked man emerges from the shadows, aiming a weapon at a target's chest at short range, received wisdom says it's time to raise hands and surrender. In some cases that may be the wisest choice. If the attacker demands a wallet, a vehicle, or valuables, hand them over and allow him to escape—but if the attacker's aim is to abduct or shoot, fighting for control of the weapon is a proposition whose odds are better than might be assumed. In scenarios based on a shooter and an unarmed target, military drills have shown that the party who makes the first move is most often the party who prevails. Even when starting from a distance of six to eight feet, unarmed targets are frequently able to run toward and disarm a shooter before he pulls the trigger—benefiting from a delayed response as the shooter processes unexpected actions.

While disarming an adversary is a high-risk maneuver, Nomads use the following protocol to increase chances of success.

Pivot and Trap the Weapon: The operative should clasp the opponent's hands and the body of the gun while pivoting his body out of the line of fire.

Drive the Barrel toward the Adversary: Twist the weapon toward the adversary's forearm.

Pull the Weapon Away: Continue to drive the barrel of the weapon over sideways while wrenching it away.

Gain Control of the Weapon: Having pried the weapon from the opponent's hands, the operative should back away quickly and do a systems check to ensure that the weapon is ready to fire. Take aim and be ready to shoot if the opponent draws a backup weapon.

No.071: Pistol Disarmament: Pointed at Chest

CONOP: Disarm adversary with pistol pointed at chest.

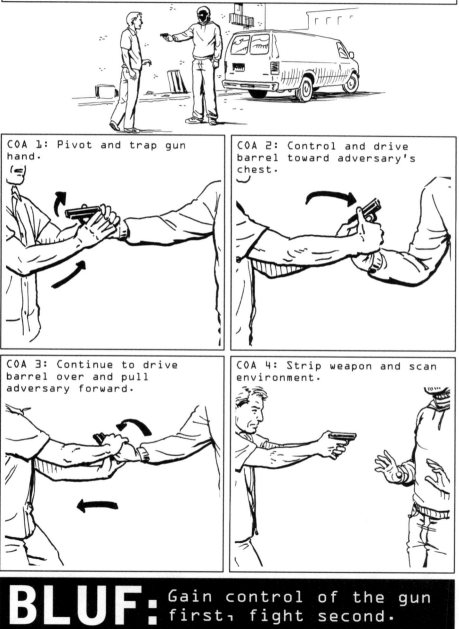

COA 1: Pivot and trap gun hand.

COA 2: Control and drive barrel toward adversary's chest.

COA 3: Continue to drive barrel over and pull adversary forward.

COA 4: Strip weapon and scan environment.

BLUF: Gain control of the gun first, fight second.

072 Pistol Disarmament: Pointed at Back

The element of surprise can be a powerful weapon. Which is why criminals tend to sneak up on their targets from behind—springing out of bushes as targets unlock their front doors, sliding out from behind parked cars as targets dig around for their keys, slinking out of the shadows as the target is mid-transaction at the corner ATM.

While an unseen weapon can cause an instinctive lock-and-freeze response, even with a gun pressed against his back, a well-trained operative *can* control the outcome of a violent altercation. If an attacker simply wants material goods, even an experienced operative may choose to hand them over and allow him to escape. The threat of kidnapping or bodily harm, on the other hand, will be met with a swift and sudden response. At the outset, the operative will push back against the weapon; on semiautomatic models, this could prevent the weapon's firing mechanism from engaging. Then, using a pivot-and-sweep motion, he will trap the weapon in his armpit in a surprisingly effective hold.

No. 072: Pistol Disarmament: Pointed at Back

CONOP: Disarm adversary with pistol pointed at back.

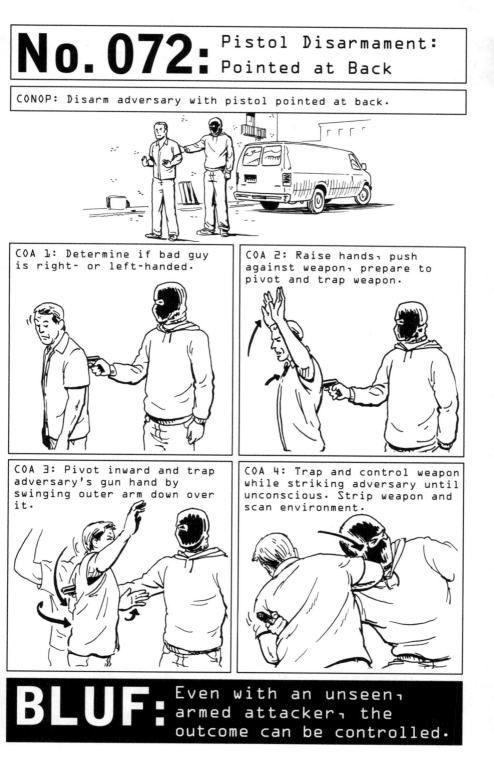

COA 1: Determine if bad guy is right- or left-handed.

COA 2: Raise hands, push against weapon, prepare to pivot and trap weapon.

COA 3: Pivot inward and trap adversary's gun hand by swinging outer arm down over it.

COA 4: Trap and control weapon while striking adversary until unconscious. Strip weapon and scan environment.

BLUF: Even with an unseen, armed attacker, the outcome can be controlled.

073 Survive an Active Shooter

Popular depictions of shooting sprees have victims (or soon-to-be victims) cowering helplessly in the face of drawn weapons, even when targets vastly outnumber the shooter or shooters. History has shown, however, that a lack of action in the face of live fire will radically reduce a target's chance of survival.

Whether they're under attack from a lone wolf or a band of terrorists, the three tactics available to civilians caught in live fire are running, hiding, and fighting. Running is the first option, and fighting is the last.

Run: If the assailant is far enough away and there appears to be an escape route immediately available, consider attempting to run. Leave belongings behind and run with a plan in mind. It is harder for a shooter to hit a moving target, so move in a zigzag pattern and/or from cover to cover.

Hide: If exiting the premises is not achievable, the next step is to find the safest area available and secure it as well as possible.

- Hide somewhere out of the assailant's view and silence cell phones and other digital devices.
- Lock the door, if possible, or create a barricade. Block the door using whatever materials are available: desks, tables, file cabinets, other furniture, books, etc. Close blinds and curtains.
- Targets should attempt to put something between themselves and the assailant. If in a room with a closed door, hide behind solid objects, away from the door. (See Identify Emergency Ballistic Shields, page 22, for preferred objects.)

No. 073: Survive an Active Shooter

CONOP: Run, hide, and fight to survive lone-wolf and terror attacks.

COA 1: RUN. Move from cover to cover.

COA 2: HIDE. Hide but don't go blind-keep eyes on the shooter.

COA 3: FIGHT. Have a plan, team up with others, be aggressive.

BLUF: Keep moving and never take eyes off the shooter.

- Call out for help using mobile devices, landlines, email, text, and radios to get first responders moving to the location.
- Place signs in exterior windows to identify the location of injured persons.
- Always consider the risk entailed by opening the door. The assailant may bang on the door, yell for help, or otherwise attempt to entice targets to open the door to a secured area.

Most ricocheting bullets follow the path of the floor, so when bullets are flying, squat or move to hands and knees rather than lying down; when taking shelter from grenades or explosives, lie on the floor with mouth open (to prevent pressure from rupturing lungs) and feet toward the explosion, with fingers interlaced behind head (to protect brain).

Fight: Fighting is an option of last resort, to be used only when all other options have failed or are unavailable. The important thing to understand, however, is that fighting *is* an option: It *is* possible for unarmed targets to effectively disarm and incapacitate an armed assailant, particularly if they outnumber him. Remember, a gun can only be shot in one direction at any one time. Attackers often assume that their targets will be cowed by the sight of their weapons; any offensive reaction is likely to catch them off guard.

Professional fight training provides advantages, but even untrained people unaccustomed to fighting can be of service, particularly if they're acting in a group in which one person or team aims to subdue or overcome the shooter's upper body and the other goes for the legs. The aim is to control the weapon and then control the shooter, getting him on the ground or knocking him out in order to escape.

Act with physical aggression and violence.

Throw anything available at the assailant.

Work as a team when with others.

Always act consciously, no matter how little time there may be.

Use improvised weapons to strike the shooter—tools, sporting goods, any hard and dense objects available. Blind the shooter with anything that burns or blinds—cleaning products, fuel, salt, pepper.

When striking, continue until the shooter has been knocked unconscious and there is no further movement—do not stop.

Related Skills: Use Improvised Body Armor, page 20; Identify Emergency Ballistic Shields, page 22; Pistol Disarmament: Pointed at Chest, page 174; Pistol Disarmament: Pointed at Back, page 176; Deliver a Devastating Elbow Strike, page 160; Strike for a Knockout, page 158; Survive a Grenade Attack, page 184.

074 Make an Improvised Gas Mask

A lachrymatory agent frequently used by law enforcement as a form of riot control, tear gas is the most common nonlethal chemical weapon in the world. Irritating the eyes, nose, throat, and skin, the substance causes debilitating short-term effects ranging from sensations of intense pain, burning, and suffocation to tears, temporary blindness, blistering, and vomiting.

But beyond the physical effects lies a potentially greater threat: Exposure to tear gas may be a precursor to mass detention. Once a crowd has been immobilized, law enforcement officials may take the opportunity to perform a round of indiscriminate arrests. Given that foreign governments sometimes use Western detainees as a form of political currency, accidentally getting caught up in such a government crackdown is a very real concern for any travelers in unstable regions.

The first tool of self-defense against violent methods of crowd control is a well-honed awareness of third-party activity. Follow common sense in generally avoiding areas where protestors congregate. If an operative passes through such an area and senses imminent chaos, he seeks to clear the premises as quickly as possible.

If he cannot avoid traveling through areas where the use of tear gas is a possibility, he will create an improvised gas mask from an empty plastic jug, a sponge, and clear packing tape.

A sponge saturated with clean water becomes an effective filter, and once taped down to the operative's face the device will act as an adequate (but not airtight) temporary gas mask.

No. 074: Make an Improvised Gas Mask

CONOP: Use milk or juice jugs to create an improvised gas mask.

COA 1: Acquire empty plastic jug or bottle, sponge, clear packing tape, and scissors.

COA 2: Cut two connected triangles and an oblong ocular slit into bottle as shown. Remove lid.

COA 3. Saturate sponge with clean water and push down into nozzle. Cover front opening with packing tape.

COA 4: Tape edges of mask to face to seal out gas.

BLUF: In moments of social unrest, the ability to evacuate the scene becomes very important.

While grenade attacks used to be relegated to active combat zones, they are increasingly a feature of surprise acts of terrorism as well as civil unrest. Though they are most often unanticipated, such attacks pose a risk that can be mitigated.

A grenade's explosion takes a predictable upside-down cone shape, generating a blast with a six-meter kill zone (depending on its model). While it may be possible for a bystander to outrun the explosion in the seconds between impact and detonation, an upright posture will leave him vulnerable to shrapnel. If cover isn't available within three steps, take one giant leap away from the grenade and to the ground. The goal is to move out of the cone-shaped explosion and away from the path of shrapnel, which rarely travels along the ground.

Position feet toward the blast in order to protect the brain. Cross legs in order to protect femoral arteries, covering ears to prevent tympanic membranes from rupturing. Keep elbows tight against the rib cage and open mouth to regularize internal and external pressure and prevent the lungs from bursting.

Know that in an urban environment, the danger of the blast will be compounded by the landscape—cement buildings and glass windows joining a litany of potential hazards. The explosion will create a secondary set of lethal projectiles from these surroundings.

No. 075: Survive a Grenade Attack

CONOP: Implement lifesaving moves when faced with live grenades.

COA 1: Is cover within three steps? If so, get behind cover.

COA 2: In the absence of cover, take two big steps away from blast and hit the deck.

COA 3. Assume proper body position.

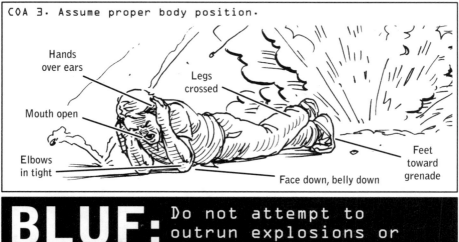

Hands over ears

Legs crossed

Mouth open

Elbows in tight

Feet toward grenade

Face down, belly down

BLUF: Do not attempt to outrun explosions or fragmentation; this is a race that cannot be won.

076 Wage Psychological Warfare

When long-term observation of a known criminal runs dry, operatives may resort to psychological warfare in order to provoke a reaction in the target.

If a target suspects his movements are being watched and has pared down his routine and contact with associates, inducing paranoia can reveal new intelligence. Who does the target call when he is feeling cornered? Breaking a pattern might reveal new behaviors or third parties for the operative to investigate.

Depending on the surveillance context, psychological warfare can involve techniques from letter drops to "soft attacks" designed primarily to provoke fear rather than create damage. Besieging a target with anonymous written communications ("We know who you are") can contribute to an overall sense of unease. Messages written as if they are coming from neighbors may convince the target that he is surrounded by an all-seeing horde of unfriendly forces—and result in his calling out to associates for assistance.

Harassing gestures may escalate to vandalism or soft attacks. Using long-range tactics such as throwing Molotov cocktails (see page 170) or scattering gunshot from a moving vehicle, operatives working alone can create the illusion that they are backed by a band of many.

The goal in psychological warfare of any sort is to distort a target's perception of reality in order to bring about a change in behavior. Stopping short of full-fledged attacks, such tactics allow the operative to remain unseen, continuing his surveillance mission from a more powerful position.

No. 076: Wage Psychological Warfare

CONOP: Battle the enemy using coercion.

COA 1: Letter Drops

COA 2: Vandalism

نحن لا نريد العيش الإرهابية بيننا

Translation: "We don't want terrorists living among us."

COA 3: Soft Attacks

BLUF: Psychological warfare can make one assailant look like many.

PART VIII

SANITIZATION: LEAVE NO TRACE

Though DNA samples can be lifted from trace quantities of mucus and sweat, the real culprits in forensic identification are human tissue and skin cells—which is why the most malevolent class of criminals and rapists will go as far as scrubbing down and shaving their entire bodies and heads in order to slough off loose skin cells and remove the possibility of being betrayed by a stray hair. (Cut hair produces variable forensic results, but cells taken from the root contain valuable genetic information.)

A thorough full-body scrub highly reduces the odds of leaving trace DNA behind, so an operative starts from the top and works his way down, brushing his hair as he washes it.

He selects clothing that covers his entire body, hot-washing it multiple times or purchasing it new. Denim and cotton are the most common fibers in the world—and therefore the least traceable. When buying clothing, he takes care not to touch it. He purchases the items next to the clothing that will actually be worn so as to avoid contact when pulling them off the rack. He applies gloves before getting dressed and wears a hat to contain his hair.

Once on target, he covers his mouth and nose with a surgical mask or a full-face ski mask to avoid the spread of saliva or mucus. He touches only what is necessary and nothing else. Attempting to clean a contaminated site is a search for a needle in a haystack—best to avoid leaving traces from the start. Once safely away from the target zone, he burns all operational clothing.

No. 077: Leave Zero DNA Behind

CONOP: Reduce the odds of leaving forensic clues behind.

COA 1: Shower and scrub entire body of loose skin and hair.

COA 2: Dress to ensure body is covered from head to toe.

COA 3: Once on target, cover mouth and nose to prevent any mucus, sweat, or tears from being distributed.

COA 4: Only touch what is necessary, nothing else.

COA 5: Burn operational clothing post-operation.

BLUF: DNA resides in skin cells—so reducing skin exposure is key to eliminating evidence.

078 Leave Zero Fingerprints Behind

As criminals and law enforcement officials know, the efficacy and frequency of fingerprint matching tends to be overstated in the popular media. A legal correlation must display a match among a dozen or more "minutiae," the ridges, whirls, and bifurcations that render each print unique—but movement and natural oils often cause smudging and other imperfections. Still, operatives take extreme measures to avoid leaving identifying evidence behind.

The key to sanitization is covering fingerprints and thoroughly cleaning tools. This is a lengthy process that lasts from the beginning of an operation to its end—for an operative who covers his tracks while on target but fails to properly sanitize his getaway vehicle or tools is an operative in danger of getting burned. As part of mission prep, he sanitizes any gear (lockpicks or weapons needed for that particular mission) by wiping it down with an acid such as paint thinner to break down oils. He thoroughly sanitizes the operational vehicle.

He also switches out gloves at each stage of the process to avoid transporting identifiable fibers or substances from the safe house to the target. In a setting where gloves would draw too much notice—retrieving information in an office or during the day—he fills in the troughs of fingerprints with superglue or files down fingerprints with a pumice stone.

Operatives seeking to erase their fingerprints over a longer period may seek to procure the chemotherapy drug Capecitabine, as pharmaceuticals are only loosely regulated in many foreign countries. As a side effect, the drug causes inflammation and blistering on the palms of hands and soles of feet, sloughing off skin cells and prints.

No. 078: Leave Zero Fingerprints Behind

CONOP: Conceal or temporarily erase fingerprints.

COA 1: Wear white cotton gloves. Fingerprints can be extracted from the inside of surgical gloves.

COA 2: Apply superglue to fingertips.

COA 3: Sand fingerprints off with pumice stone.

COA 4: Take Capecitabine to achieve the side effect of fingerprint loss.

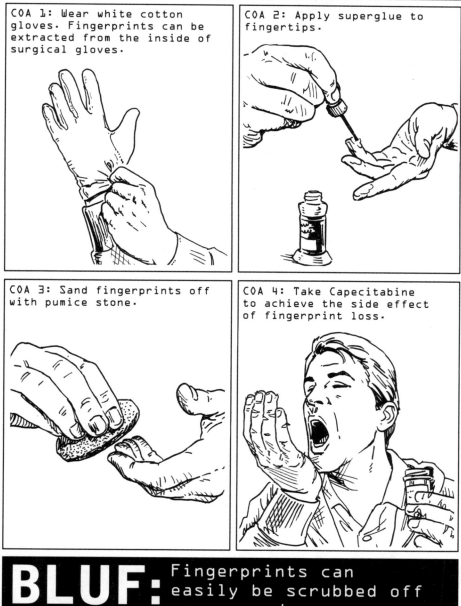

BLUF: Fingerprints can easily be scrubbed off or covered.

079 Leave Zero Digital Trace Behind

The most dangerous element in any given environment may be the device found in the pants pocket of the majority of civilians in the developed world: a cellular phone, an electronic tether that could be employed to track a target's every move. This inadvertent digital scrapbook can also be used to create a detailed biography—including not only access to bank accounts but also information about family and friends.

In areas where communications companies are owned and operated by host-nation governments, digital security becomes particularly relevant. Any foreign phones pop up on cellular networks as outsider devices, and as such, become increasingly vulnerable to being tracked. When possible, operatives prefer to purchase prepaid, contract-free phones inside the host nation rather than bringing in their own.

In the event that they do travel with electronics, operatives protect them by either shielding or fully disabling them. Cell phones, tablets, and laptops can be shielded from both incoming and outgoing signals by a pocket made out of a quadruple layer of aluminum foil. (Smart devices will plow through single or double layers by redirecting all of their batteries' energies toward finding a signal.) The foil must be tightly compacted around the device, leaving no gaps.

A more polished option is a discreet shielded carrying case (e.g., Zero Trace) embedded with a double layer of metal fabric that blocks all signals, in observance of CIA protocol.

Because many cell phones employ small backup batteries that run even when phones are turned off, in the absence of a workable shield, removing *all* batteries and SIM cards is the only way to render a phone completely safe from any vulnerabilities. As this isn't possible on some phones, sometimes the only option is to leave the device behind.

No. 079: Leave Zero Digital Trace Behind

CONOP: Prevent remote hacking and tracking.

COA 1: Build a four-layer aluminum-foil pocket to block all incoming and outgoing signals.

COA 2: Use shielded products (Zero Trace) to block all incoming and outgoing signals.

COA 3: OFF is not really OFF—remove all batteries and SIM cards from phones, tablets, and laptops.

COA 4: Leave phone and other digital tech at home.

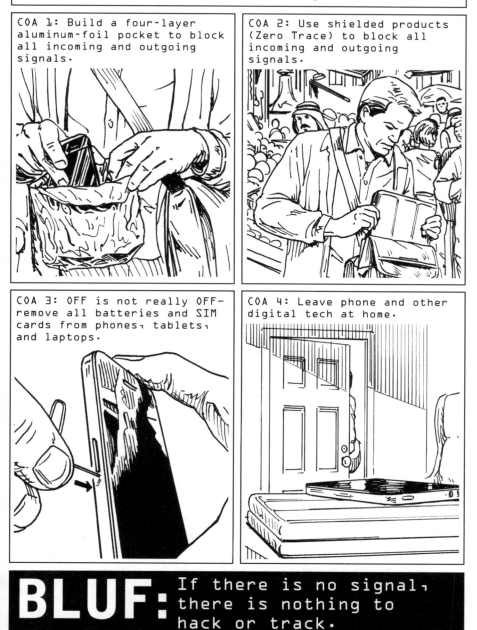

BLUF: If there is no signal, there is nothing to hack or track.

080 Trick Facial Recognition Software

Forged identification papers grant an active Nomad an important layer of anonymity—but if he has already been identified by foreign governments as a probable security risk, his picture may come up in a database at border crossings or other high-security checkpoints. Current facial recognition software, based on imagery, is still relatively easy to bypass, so the Nomad will proceed as planned.

Using algorithms that compare particular anchor points within a given database of images—noses, the space between eyes, the size of each eye, the shape of cheekbones, chins, and ears—the technology focuses on distinctive bony prominences that cannot be readily altered. But covering up or otherwise obfuscating those anchor points leaves the software little to work with.

Large sunglasses and long bangs can be used to cover the forehead, brow bone, and part of the cheekbones. A hat pulled down low and a downward-tilted head can throw an operative's face into shadow. Smiling changes the shape of the eyes and pushes tissue over the cheekbones, which is why many countries require a neutral facial expression in passport photos.

Frequently in use in Las Vegas casinos, where it prevents cheating gamblers from siphoning off millions of dollars in revenue, facial recognition is an ever-evolving science. As social media platforms begin to use it to tag and sort through images, it will only grow more and more sophisticated. One day facial recognition will be a well-oiled mechanism utilized to secure anything from border crossings and ATMs to private homes and businesses, along with the up-and-coming vascular identification technologies that take thermal pictures of human faces, using the positioning of facial veins and arteries as the basis for identification and leaving few if any options for subterfuge. But for now, the technology leaves plenty of gaps for a Nomad to exploit.

No. 080: Trick Facial Recognition Software

CONOP: Prevent identification via facial recognition software.

COA 1: Wear a ball cap and keep head tilted down.

COA 2: Wear a light disguise.

COA 3: Check databases for incriminating images.

BLUF: Facial recognition software based on bone structure can be tricked by the simple act of smiling.

081 Trick Fingerprint Scanning Software

The most widely used form of biometrics, fingerprinting is increasingly traveling from the criminal justice system into the realm of consumer electronics. Harnessed for such uses as unlocking smartphones, authorizing payments, and securing doors or safes, the technology is becoming more widespread. As it does, its quality becomes more variable, displaying vulnerabilities for Nomads and common criminals to exploit.

For an operative, collecting fingerprints is frequently a postmortem scenario. Performing "battle damage assessment" in the aftermath of a planned event such as an explosion, he might be tasked with gathering biometric information in order to confirm the target's identity. In such cases the operative will go the most direct route: severing the target's thumb.

But thumbprints can be replicated via less violent means, one of which involves the chewy candy known as the gummy bear. Malleable and tacky, gummy bears are exceptionally receptive to fingerprints. Because they have a consistency similar to that of human tissue, they are also well-suited to deceiving lower-quality fingerprint scanning mechanisms.

Cheap scanners don't read depth, which is why they won't register the fact that a fingerprint's textural pattern has been reversed—the ridges turned into valleys, and vice versa, as they are transferred onto the gummy bear. When confronted with more sophisticated technology, Nomads use a combination of Silly Putty and gelatin, impressioning the Silly Putty, then pouring a gelatin solution into the clay and letting it sit until it gels. Carefully removing the gel nets a duplicate fingerprint that's a match for pattern and is impressioned to proper depth.

No. 081: Trick Fingerprint Scanning Software

CONOP: Accurately impression target fingerprints in order to gain access to target safes, phones, and other fingerprint-protected devices.

COA 1: Roll small piece of Silly Putty or model clay into a ball, and press into target finger.

COA 2: Refrigerate or freeze putty.

COA 3: Make extra-thick gelatin.

COA 4: Once gelatin has cooled to thick gel, melt it in microwave, then let cool to a gel again. Repeat until the gelatin has no bubbles and a drop acts thick and rubbery.

COA 5: Once gelatin is rubbery and bubble-free, melt once more, then pour hot liquid gelatin into putty fingerprint mold.

COA 6: Place putty and gelatin in freezer. Within a few minutes, gelatin should harden into solid, rubbery substance. Peel gelatin carefully away from putty to yield a working gelatin fingertip.

BLUF: Fingerprints are unique—but easily replicated if left unattended.

082 Create a Hasty Disguise

In the real world of covert operations, disguise doesn't follow the well-worn conceits of spy movies and thrillers—the bathroom dye job, the use of masks. Instead, an effective and rapid transformation relies on illusion, employing tricks of perception rather than true disguise. A few props can turn a businessman into a service worker, and a change in color pattern can cause a target to vanish from sight.

In attempting to evade surveillance teams, operatives employ a working knowledge of surveillance psychology. What does a surveillance team actually *see* when they're watching a target? Particularly when watching from a distance, a surveillance team will home in on color blocks rather than facial features or hairstyle, using broad visual strokes to keep track of the target's movements. Over time, the colors of the target's clothing become ingrained in the surveillance team's brain—instead of scanning for the target, they unconsciously scan for the colors he's wearing. An easy way to subvert their expectations is to duck into a public restroom or fitting room and very quickly switch out to different colors. If wearing white over denim, switch to black over denim and walk right out the door without being spotted.

Another way to manipulate the expectations of a surveillance team is to start out in bright colors. This will cause the team to relax, secure in the knowledge that they are watching an easy mark. When the operative emerges from a stopping point in a muted outfit, he'll be as good as invisible.

No. 082: Create a Hasty Disguise

CONOP: Elude pursuers using the simplest form of subterfuge.

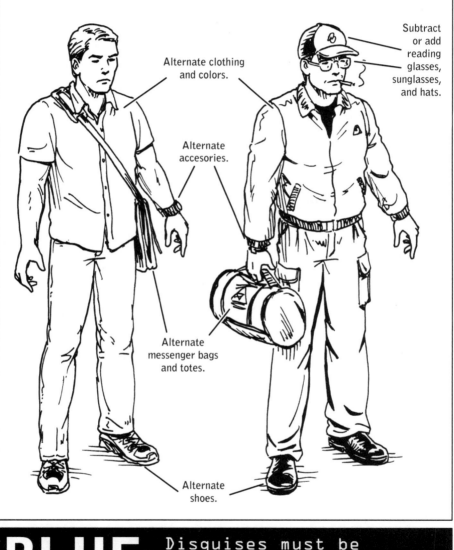

Subtract or add reading glasses, sunglasses, and hats.

Alternate clothing and colors.

Alternate accesories.

Alternate messenger bags and totes.

Alternate shoes.

BLUF: Disguises must be explainable–wigs and fake mustaches will lead straight to jail.

083 Get Past a Guard Dog

When Nomads write up a reconnaissance report on a target's home or business, they always include a full accounting of any animals they come across. Even untrained dogs, when spooked, can give away a Nomad's location or alert an owner to the fact that something out of the ordinary is under way. Any infiltration plan must include measures for distracting or subduing pets or guard dogs while the Nomad goes about his business—and particularly in third-world countries, operatives must also be wary of the wild dogs that roam the streets in packs.

Killing guard dogs leaves behind a trail of unwanted evidence, so Nomads resort to tactics that temporarily disable or distract the animal. A canine deterrent spray, equivalent to pepper spray, will irritate a dog's eyes and carries a smell that dogs find extremely unpleasant. A burst of compressed air (the product used to dust electronics) will freeze a dog's nose and have him running for cover. Compressed to fluid form, the mixture of nitrogen and other gasses undergoes a massive drop in temperature upon being released from the can; when emitted from a can that is turned upside down, the gas will spray out as liquid and immediately freeze to ice.

Though challenging to come by in any scenario, female dog urine is one of the most effective canine distraction tools in a Nomad's arsenal. Sprayed in a dog's face or away from the entry point, its scent proves an irresistible enticement for any attack dog, no matter how well trained.

CONOP: Temporarily disable or distract a guard dog.

COA 1: 50/50 Solution Ammonia/Water-spray in dog's face.

COA 2: Compressed Air-freeze dog's nose with keyboard air cleaner.

COA 3: Female Dog Urine-spray in dog's face or away from entry point.

BLUF: Killing a guard dog leaves behind a trail of unwanted evidence.

084 Discreetly Clear a Flooded Scuba Mask

To operatives carrying out missions with complex logistics, diving is just another form of clandestine movement—one that is well known to the drug cartels that move thousands of kilograms of contraband across the world via submarine (the ocean floor being nearly impossible to police).

While swimming across open waters runs the risk of detection, diving keeps the operative concealed deep underwater, giving him a stealthy way to attack boats, piers, and bridges. It's also an unexpected means of escape. Upon accessing a cache of scuba gear submerged at a predetermined location (see page 38), a Violent Nomad could disappear forever with a single breath-hold.

Scuba diving's flexibility comes with its fair share of vulnerabilities. Entry and exit pose complex logistical challenges, and medical hazards are abundant, especially for an operative diving alone. Typically, a Nomad cannot stay underwater for longer than three hours, so any tactical plan must account for this limitation.

Though the risk of detection diminishes once the operative is underwater, one telltale sign of activity—easily observed in a quiet harbor—is the trail of bubbles emitted by the overly hasty clearing of a scuba mask.

No. 084: Discreetly Clear a Flooded Scuba Mask

CONOP: Clear a flooded scuba mask without creating bubbles.

COA 1: Tilt head so water pools at the bottom of the mask.

COA 2: Use the heel of hand to put pressure on the upper side of the mask, reinforcing the seal.

COA 3: With the opposite hand, pinch the seal of the mask closest to cheek bone and mouth to create an opening.

COA 4: Exhale slowly through nose. The water level will start to drop as water exits via the pinched opening.

COA 5: If bubbles escape, quickly fan them with hand to break them up.

BLUF: Bubbles create an aquatic footprint for the enemy to follow. Never let them get to the surface.

085 Dispose of a Body

With a preference for vehicular collisions and untraceable injections, a Violent Nomad always attempts to disguise an assassination so that it looks like an accident. But sometimes a hit simply goes bad. A Nomad makes mistakes that could lead to his identification or is surprised mid-mission by an incidental third party.

In order to safely extricate himself from the area of operation, the Nomad must first dispose of the corpse.

Land Burial: Compared to a typical horizontal burial site, a vertical grave leaves a significantly smaller footprint aboveground—and less surface area means a smaller signature for dogs to sniff out. The grave is dug two feet deeper than the length of the body, which is lowered down headfirst so that organs (which give off the most scent) are buried deep underground.

Thermal Burial: To eradicate all trace of a body, a cremation chamber can be replicated by filling a fifty-gallon steel drum halfway full with jet fuel. (Jet fuel can be commandeered from small private airports with minimal security.) After about two hours, bones and teeth will have turned to dust, making any identification near impossible. This method will give off a significant amount of smoke (more easily spotted during the day) and flame (more easily spotted at night) and must be undertaken in desolate, rural environments.

Maritime Burial: The least discoverable burial site is a watery grave at the bottom of the ocean floor, a few nautical miles offshore. Weighted down by fifty pounds of steel pipe, bricks, or cinder blocks, the body is wrapped in a layer of perforated construction plastic or ground cloth so that air bubbles won't prevent it from sinking. An operative will secure the plastic with a double layer of chicken wire to prevent body parts from floating to the surface as the body is attacked by marine life or degrades over time.

No. 085: Dispose of a Body

CONOP: Ensure a body can never be found.

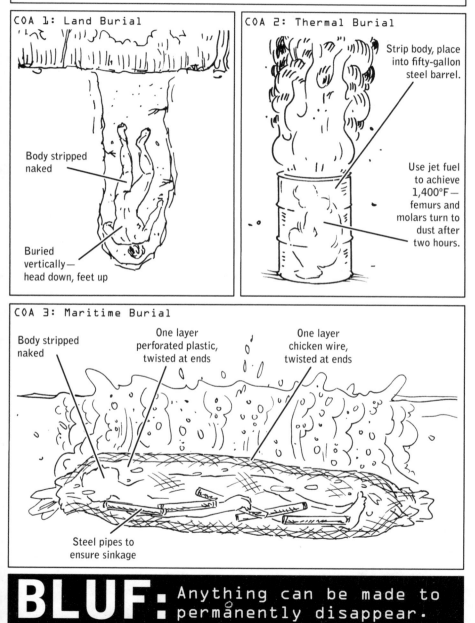

COA 1: Land Burial

Body stripped naked

Buried vertically— head down, feet up

COA 2: Thermal Burial

Strip body, place into fifty-gallon steel barrel.

Use jet fuel to achieve 1,400°F— femurs and molars turn to dust after two hours.

COA 3: Maritime Burial

Body stripped naked

One layer perforated plastic, twisted at ends

One layer chicken wire, twisted at ends

Steel pipes to ensure sinkage

BLUF: Anything can be made to permanently disappear.

PART IX

EXFILTRATION AND ESCAPE: HOW TO DISAPPEAR

086 Create a Rappelling Harness

Combined with an improvised rope (see page 212) a rappelling harness made out of a single bedsheet could be the key to a safe and fast escape. For an operative, it may also allow for access to a target's room from a building facade. Once the mission has been executed, the operative vanishes and the sheet is discarded—an untraceable, anonymous artifact swiped from a hotel room or purchased under an assumed name.

A king-size sheet will create a harness large enough for adults, while full-size sheets can be used to create harnesses for children. A similar harness can be made from materials such as one-inch-wide tubular nylon, cargo straps, furniture covers, and the plastic sheeting used in commercial construction. An important additional layer of safety during rope descents, the harness ensures that an operative won't fall to his death if he loses hold of the rope. Relatively safe, secure, and easy to make in less than three minutes, it provides three "points of failure"; when secured to an improvised rope, gravity and tension should ensure that if one loop fails, the other two will continue to hold.

A secure knot and proper rope length are key to a safe rappelling apparatus. A rope that is too long negates the purpose of the harness, which should allow the Nomad to "bounce" (as if from a bungee cord) a few feet from the ground in the event that he loses hold of the rope. In building the rope, use a guideline of one sheet per story.

Related Skills: Escape a Multistory Building, page 212.

No. 086: Create a Rappelling Harness

CONOP: Improvise a rappelling harness using a bedsheet.

COA 1: A king-size sheet will provide the length needed for an adult harness.

COA 2: Fold in half diagonally, then roll sheet.

COA 3: Use a square knot to tie both ends together. Shape the loop into a triangle on the floor.

Square knot

COA 4: Straddle triangle with apex pointing forward.

COA 5: Pull harness up between legs and around waist.

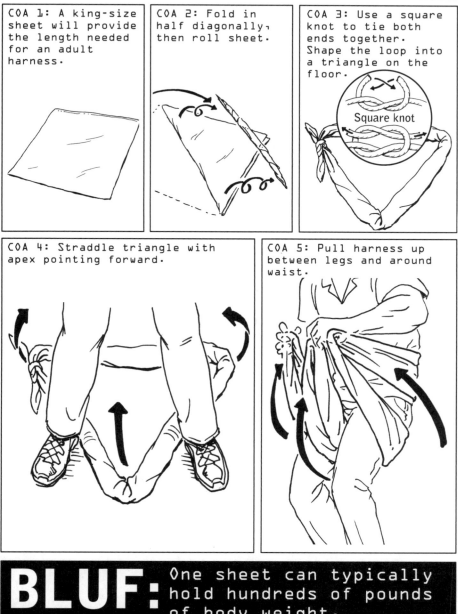

BLUF: One sheet can typically hold hundreds of pounds of body weight.

The action heroes of the silver screen can be seen scaling the face of skyscrapers using all manner of futuristic suction devices and laser-cutting rappelling techniques. In the real world of covert operations, however, an escape from a multistory building is likely to be assisted by a much more humble prop: an ordinary bedsheet. Whether escaping a fire, a hostage situation, or the scene of a crime, learning to create a dependable rope out of bedsheets will ensure a swift exit from a multistory building, under any set of circumstances. Stronger than some ropes, high-thread-count sheets represent another case in which improvised materials can perform with greater effectiveness than their store-bought counterparts: One sheet may hold hundreds of pounds of body weight. (Tensile strength increases with thread count, and an increase in tensile strength can handle more weight.)

When checking into a hotel room, opt for a king-size bed—king-size sheets mean more material, which translates into additional rope length. Once checked in, call the front desk and request additional sheets in order to gather enough rope length to make a potential descent. Building stories are approximately ten feet tall, and one king-size sheet should provide twelve feet of length.

Tensile strength aside, the rope will only be as dependable as the anchor to which it is tied. The chosen anchor should either be permanently affixed to walls, larger than the window, or heavier than the person it is holding—beds, radiators, large dressers or tables, and heavy couches are all good options. In the absence of those possibilities, a chair wedged behind a closed door may do the trick.

Tie the sheets together using square knots, which tighten under stress, and always leave at least six inches to one foot of length at the knot ends. If escaping fire, wet the sheets prior to tying them and make sure the anchor isn't highly flammable. For added security, pair rope with the improvised rappelling harness, page 210.

No. 087: Escape a Multistory Building

CONOP: Use bedsheets to climb down a multistory building.

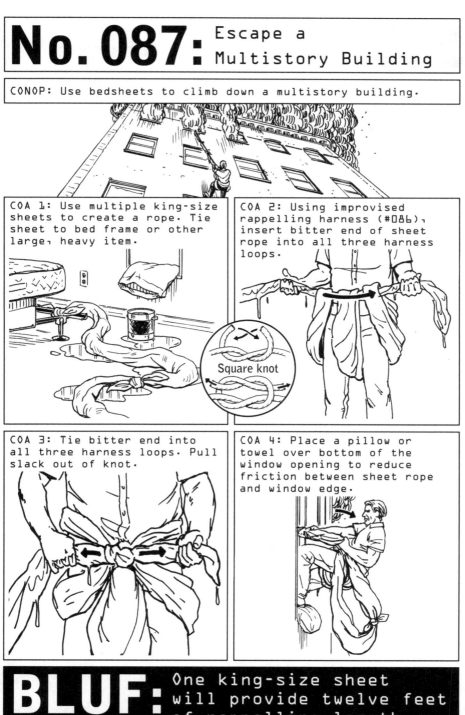

COA 1: Use multiple king-size sheets to create a rope. Tie sheet to bed frame or other large, heavy item.

Square knot

COA 2: Using improvised rappelling harness (#086), insert bitter end of sheet rope into all three harness loops.

COA 3: Tie bitter end into all three harness loops. Pull slack out of knot.

COA 4: Place a pillow or towel over bottom of the window opening to reduce friction between sheet rope and window edge.

BLUF: One king-size sheet will provide twelve feet of rappelling length.

088 Survive a Drowning Attempt

When an operative is captured in hostile territory, the odds of survival are low. Instead of being taken to trial, he will likely simply be made to "disappear"—which is why operatives practice escaping while wearing undefeatable restraints on hands and feet, both in water and on land. Tied up, thrown into open waters, and left to drown to death, the well-trained operative still has recourse to a few skills that can help extend his life until he is found or reaches solid ground.

When it comes to self-preservation in water, the key to survival is breath control. With the lungs full of air, the human body is buoyant—so deep breaths and quick exhales are key. Buoyancy in freshwater is more challenging but still achievable. Panicking, which can lead to hyperventilation, is the number-one enemy to survival.

Restraints and body positioning may make breathing a challenge, but repositioning is always within the Nomad's grasp. In shallow waters, use a sinking and bouncing approach (see diagram) to travel toward shore, ricocheting off the seabed or lake floor up to the surface for an inhale.

When facing down, whether floating in place or using a backward kicking motion to swim to shore, the operative should arch his back in order to raise his head above water.

In rough seas, this may not give him enough clearance to get his head out of the water. Instead, a full body rotation will allow him to take a deep breath and then continue traveling forward.

No. 088: Survive a Drowning Attempt

CONOP: Prevent drowning when restrained in deep waters.

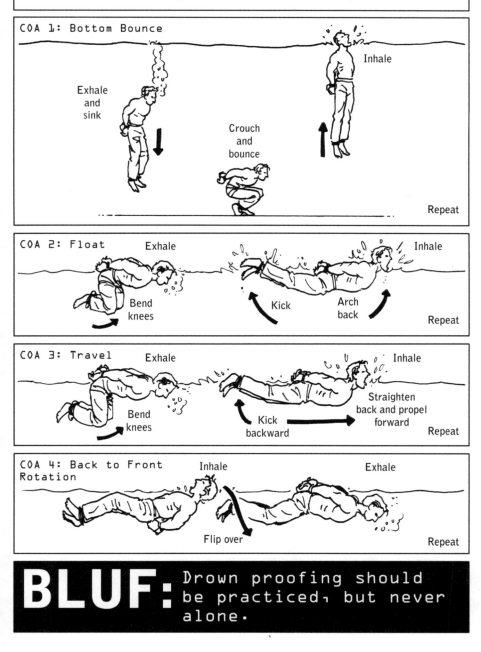

COA 1: Bottom Bounce

Exhale and sink

Inhale

Crouch and bounce

Repeat

COA 2: Float

Exhale

Inhale

Bend knees

Kick

Arch back

Repeat

COA 3: Travel

Exhale

Inhale

Bend knees

Kick backward

Straighten back and propel forward

Repeat

COA 4: Back to Front Rotation

Inhale

Exhale

Flip over

Repeat

BLUF: Drown proofing should be practiced, but never alone.

089 Escape from an Automobile Trunk

Violent Nomads frequently operate in or near countries that are at war or in political crisis, and thus are vulnerable to being kidnapped for ransom—sometimes as a calculated attempt to thwart a mission, sometimes simply as a result of being in the wrong place at the wrong time. More and more frequently, travelers to unstable regions face the same risk.

The most predictable points of vulnerability in a traveler's schedule are his departure from and return to his hotel at the beginning and end of his day—but an abduction may also be the result of a staged automobile accident. Common ruses used by kidnappers to apprehend a target on the road include:

The Bump: The attacker bumps the target's vehicle from behind. The target gets out to assess the damage and suddenly finds himself in the trunk of a car.

The Good Samaritan: The attackers stage what appears to be an accident or feign a car problem. The target stops to assist and suddenly finds himself in the trunk of a car.

The Trap: Kidnappers use surveillance to follow the target home. When he pulls into his driveway and waits for the gate to open, the attacker pulls up from behind and blocks his car. The target finds himself in the trunk of a car.

In each of these scenarios, the target ends up imprisoned. But he doesn't have to remain in that state. Take the time to understand how a vehicle's trunk operates, learning its vulnerabilities and how to defeat them. If locked in a trunk, always try to be positioned in a way that allows access to escape tools.

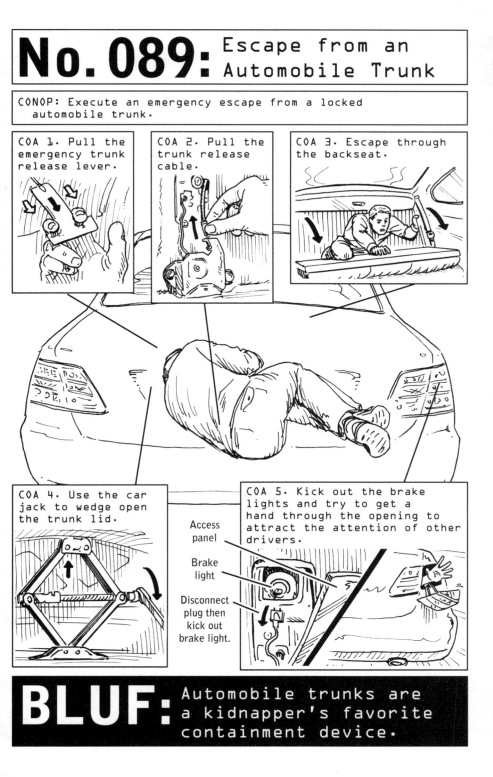

No. 089: Escape from an Automobile Trunk

CONOP: Execute an emergency escape from a locked automobile trunk.

COA 1. Pull the emergency trunk release lever.

COA 2. Pull the trunk release cable.

COA 3. Escape through the backseat.

COA 4. Use the car jack to wedge open the trunk lid.

COA 5. Kick out the brake lights and try to get a hand through the opening to attract the attention of other drivers.

Access panel

Brake light

Disconnect plug then kick out brake light.

BLUF: Automobile trunks are a kidnapper's favorite containment device.

090 Develop a Bug-Out Route

While a well-concealed cache of escape tools is an essential component of mission prep (see page 16), the most vital tool of escape isn't a shim or a compass but a meticulously planned emergency route. When unexpected developments arise, operatives *must* be able to ensure their own safe exit out of an area of operation they never officially breached.

Planning primary and alternate escape routes is a weeks- or even months-long endeavor that requires the development of a significant amount of area knowledge. Operatives canvass roads to determine the quickest and most discreet routes of escape. They use a thorough research process that identifies friendly and unfriendly areas—and assume they are at risk of being followed, ambushed, or chased. They look for routes least likely to be observed by third parties or to include dead ends, checkpoints, or choke points. And they create bridges from their primary route to their alternate routes, building a network of secondary branches they can veer into in the event that they are followed or encounter unexpected roadblocks.

Once they've established their routes, operatives identify temporary lodging or hide sites—stopping points that will enable them to travel by night and rest by day. Using detailed calculations based on mileage, speed, and the availability of supplies in surrounding areas, they stage caches of food, water, and life support at predetermined points along the routes. They may hide alternate vehicles at cache points in order to shake off potential tails or set up rally points where they'll meet known associates to hand off intelligence or other assets.

Loaded into a password-protected GPS that is stashed in the operative's bolt bag, the bug-out routes provide an effective form of operational insurance. The more complex and detailed they are, the better—emergency exfiltration is one of the many areas in which research and attention to detail can win out over brute force and even the most well-armed pursuers.

No. 090: Develop a Bug-Out Route

CONOP: Plan emergency escape routes to prevent capture.

COA 1: Research avenues of escape where movement can be broken down into rally points, cache points, modes of transportation (foot to mobile to public transportation), and temporary lodging/hiding.

COA 2: Develop primary and alternate routes.

Starting Point(s)
End Point(s)
Rally Point(s) (preplanned locations where you'll meet up with someone along the route)
Go Point(s) (friendly locations such as the homes of associates, hospitals, known remote locations)
No-Go Point(s) (unfriendly locations such as bad neighborhoods, places with no life support such as food and water)
Choke Point(s) (places where you could be ambushed)
Water Crossings
Towns
Fuel, Water, and Food
Terrain Association Marker(s) (locations or objects such as water towers that will help you figure out exactly where you are once you're on the ground)

COA 3: Load and conceal life-support caches along routes.

COA 4: Load routes and stopping points into a personal GPS.

COA 5: Password-protect and conceal GPS in bolt bag.

BLUF: Clearing the area of operation is an integral part of the mission.

091 Perform a J-turn

Only in the movies do operatives routinely drive through barricades, off of bridges, and onto the wrong side of highways. In reality, high-octane vehicular maneuvers are rarely deployed in the field. In most cases, escalating a tense situation into a chase is a tactical disaster; engaging in a highly conspicuous maneuver when it isn't warranted only gives the adversary reason to come after the operative.

Still, there are times when properly executed evasion techniques can mean the difference between mission success and detention—which is why Nomads regularly rehearse them in abandoned parking lots or on untraveled rural roads prior to an operation.

The J-turn, Forward 180, or "Bootleg Turn" allows a Nomad to quickly shift the momentum of the vehicle from one direction of travel to another within the width of a two-lane road. To properly perform a J-turn, the Nomad must first master the vehicle's braking systems. The initial attempt is never made during a crisis.

The coordinated use of the emergency brake and release is essential for the maneuver, keeping the vehicle under control by "locking up" the rear brakes. Avoiding the use of the foot brake prevents the front tires from sliding or skidding and wards off a loss of momentum by the keeping the heavy, engine-bearing front of the vehicle from degrading and "sinking"—an effect which would prevent the vehicle from pivoting.

The steering wheel must be turned quickly and aggressively. As the car rotates a full 180 degrees, remove left foot from the emergency brake and use right foot to press the accelerator. To prevent the tires from rolling off the rims, ensure tire pressure is a minimum of five to ten pounds per square inch over max pressure limits. Since every vehicle is different, speeds must be greatly reduced when conducting maneuvers in high-center-of-gravity vehicles such as trucks or SUVs. Even for trained drivers any speed greater than thirty-five miles per hour may result in flipping the vehicle and should be avoided.

No. 091: Perform a J-turn

CONOP: Quickly reverse the direction of travel on a narrow road.

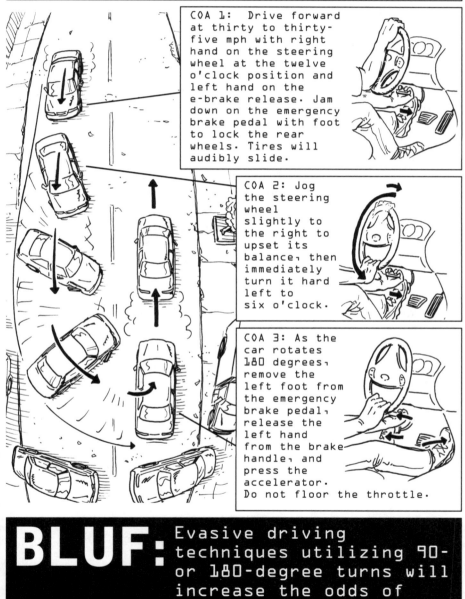

COA 1: Drive forward at thirty to thirty-five mph with right hand on the steering wheel at the twelve o'clock position and left hand on the e-brake release. Jam down on the emergency brake pedal with foot to lock the rear wheels. Tires will audibly slide.

COA 2: Jog the steering wheel slightly to the right to upset its balance, then immediately turn it hard left to six o'clock.

COA 3: As the car rotates 180 degrees, remove the left foot from the emergency brake pedal, release the left hand from the brake handle, and press the accelerator. Do not floor the throttle.

BLUF: Evasive driving techniques utilizing 90- or 180-degree turns will increase the odds of escape.

092 Perform a Reverse 180

When time is of the essence, a cumbersome U-turn is not the best tool in an operative's arsenal. U-turns always involve the risk of becoming time-intensive three-point turns; at a high speed, they can also result in popping a tire on the curb or driving off the road. In an attack situation, a Reverse 180 is the fastest way to reverse the direction of travel—but the maneuver should be attempted only in extreme emergency, by highly skilled drivers when under imminent, life-threatening danger. Performed incorrectly, a Reverse 180 could flip a vehicle or permanently damage its transmission.

The turn should be performed at speeds no greater than thirty miles per hour. Emergency brakes must be in good working order, and a seat belt must be used. Though in order to reduce friction the move is best performed on wet or slippery surfaces, in any environment it produces a stress that cars are not designed to accept. In other words, the Reverse 180 is not to be taken lightly.

Reverse: Starting from a complete stop, shift into reverse and drive backward for three car lengths. Stay under twenty-five miles per hour.

Turn the Wheel: Shift gears to neutral, remove foot from the gas pedal, and yank the wheel all the way to the left as quickly as possible.

Hold the Wheel in Place: Hold the wheel in place until the vehicle has completed a 180-degree turn. Do not brake.

Accelerate: Shift back into drive and accelerate away from attackers.

Note: If attempting an escape on a road that does not allow sufficient width to attempt the turn, driving in reverse in a slalom pattern will help handicap the attackers' aim.

No. 092: Perform a Reverse 180

CONOP: Master an essential defensive driving escape skill.

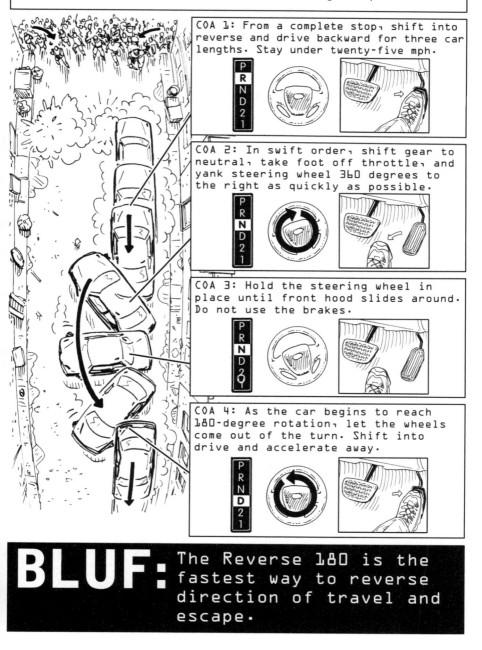

COA 1: From a complete stop, shift into reverse and drive backward for three car lengths. Stay under twenty-five mph.

COA 2: In swift order, shift gear to neutral, take foot off throttle, and yank steering wheel 360 degrees to the right as quickly as possible.

COA 3: Hold the steering wheel in place until front hood slides around. Do not use the brakes.

COA 4: As the car begins to reach 180-degree rotation, let the wheels come out of the turn. Shift into drive and accelerate away.

BLUF: The Reverse 180 is the fastest way to reverse direction of travel and escape.

093 Survive Vehicular Impact

Due to their propensity for high-risk defensive and offensive driving techniques, operatives have a tendency to fall victim to a higher-than-average rate of vehicular accidents. Surviving these accidents while minimizing stress on the body is a matter of advance preparation and postural know-how—techniques that apply to any civilian caught in a car crash, whether as a result of a high-speed escape or a run-of-the-mill incident.

While the ability to survive a crash might appear to qualify as defensive knowledge rather than a "deadly" skill, self-preservation in the face of accidents or attempted assaults is key to mission success. In order to remain deadly, a Violent Nomad must remain safe.

One of the most commonly used steering positions—controlling the wheel with a hand placed at twelve o'clock—is also the most dangerous. On impact, such positioning assures that when the airbag activates, it will violently thrust an operative's forearm into his face. Proper steering positioning (see illustration) may both prevent the operative from ending up with a forearm full of teeth and protect his thumbs from breaking.

For passengers, bracing during impact is a simple but lifesaving technique that can significantly reduce the risk of spinal and brain injuries. (Seat belts adequately restrain shoulders and hips but cannot prevent heads from flying forward due to crash momentum.) In one accident involving a small aircraft, passengers were sleeping when the plane collided with a stand of trees. One passenger out of the sixteen awoke and braced for impact, and he was the lone survivor.

If using the vehicle for a planned impact such as a PIT, disengage the airbags so that they don't impede escape.

No. 093: Survive Vehicular Impact

CONOP: Proper procedures for surviving vehicular impact.

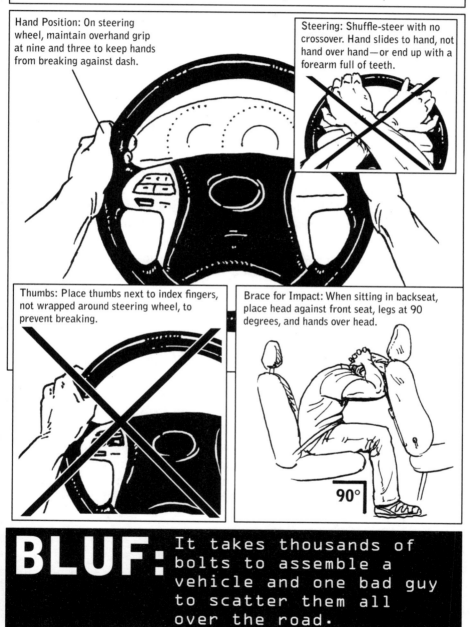

Hand Position: On steering wheel, maintain overhand grip at nine and three to keep hands from breaking against dash.

Steering: Shuffle-steer with no crossover. Hand slides to hand, not hand over hand—or end up with a forearm full of teeth.

Thumbs: Place thumbs next to index fingers, not wrapped around steering wheel, to prevent breaking.

Brace for Impact: When sitting in backseat, place head against front seat, legs at 90 degrees, and hands over head.

90°

BLUF: It takes thousands of bolts to assemble a vehicle and one bad guy to scatter them all over the road.

094 Break Through a Two-Car Block

Checkpoints or roadblocks are common sights in many parts of the world. Foreign governments rely on them to deter crime or terrorist insurrections, particularly after nightfall—but the deep cover of night is also a prime time for bad guys to set up false checkpoints Determining whether a checkpoint is legitimate or a terrorist ruse can be a question of survival, one that relies heavily on instinct and split-second decision-making. If the Nomad believes the checkpoint to be hostile, he will first check to see if he can accomplish a discreet evasion to avoid the roadblock. If he cannot, breaking through the roadblock may be his best bet.

Many checkpoints use cars as barriers in order to funnel traffic into a single line; one guard interrogates drivers as they stop, while the second remains in one of the obstructing vehicles and backs out of the way when a car is allowed to pass. If hit in the right place, the blocking vehicle is relatively easy to "move." The momentum of a full-size car traveling at ten to twenty miles per hour will almost effortlessly cause the obstructing vehicle to spin out of the way while inflicting only minimum damage to the operative's vehicle.

Aim for a push, not a collision. If traveling at highway speeds, slow down significantly or come to a stop before "pushing" the obstructing vehicle out of the way. One car length is all that is needed. Control the angle of impact so that the front right or left corners of the vehicle makes contact with the front axle of the blocking car, protecting radiator and engine components (see diagram). Significant damage incurred to the vehicle will defeat the likelihood of an escape.

No. 094: Break Through a Two-Car Block

CONOP: Safely drive through an enemy roadblock.

COA 1: Stop one car length away, positioning vehicle in the middle of the road.

Aim at front axles.

COA 2: When the standing guard approaches driver's side window, floor the accelerator pedal and aim front fender at the front axle of one of the blocking vehicles.

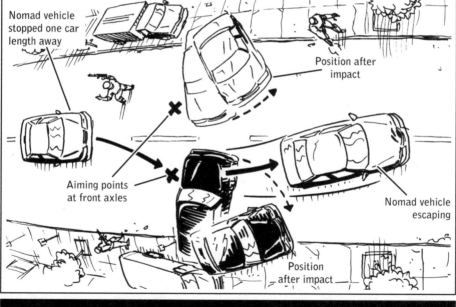

Nomad vehicle stopped one car length away

Position after impact

Aiming points at front axles

Nomad vehicle escaping

Position after impact

BLUF: Only ram a roadblock if it's a choice between action and detention or death.

095 Escape an Ambush

Where do the greatest dangers lurk? For Violent Nomads and civilians alike, it's the unseen menaces that pose the most peril—which is why violent attackers so often strike from concealed positions, using the elements of speed, stealth, and surprise to catch their targets off guard. From dense underbrush to desolate intersections and dark corners, attackers choose ambush spots that enable them to strike rapidly, carry out their mission, and disappear without alerting potential third parties.

Operatives know that the best defense against targeted ambushes is to constantly vary routes and habits. Take varying routes to and from work. Change up departure times. Criminals and kidnappers frequently stalk their marks, plotting attacks around the vulnerabilities in their routines. Foil them by being unpredictable.

Cultivate a constant awareness of possible ambush sites and scenarios. Look out for desolate areas, choke points where roads narrow, and any structures or landmarks that could provide cover for potential assailants. If possible, plan routes to avoid potential ambush points. The simplest way to defeat an ambush is to sidestep the threat completely.

If an operative cannot avoid or anticipate a potential ambush point, he should increase his speed as he approaches. Particularly when driving, he may be able to speed through the ambush point and back onto a less isolated stretch of road before the attacker is able to make contact.

The attacker is counting on the element of surprise in order to overwhelm the target. If the target can get a head start by anticipating the attacker—despite not being able to see him—he will remove one of the attacker's primary advantages.

No. 095: Escape an Ambush

CONOP: Understand and identify ambush points (marked by Xs) and avoid them.

COA 1: Identify areas where speed, stealth, and surprise exist.

COA 2: Plan routes and times around possible Xs.

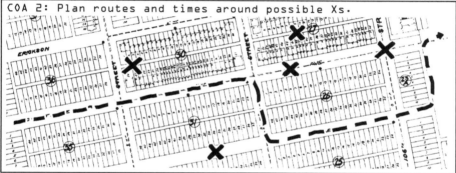

COA 3: No alternate routes available? Stay alert, move quickly through ambush zones, and have an exit strategy.

BLUF: Without the element of surprise, an ambush will be reduced to a fight.

ESCAPE ABDUCTION

In the face of abduction attempts, the old adage rings true: Never follow an attacker to a second location. But sometimes an operative will be outnumbered, outgunned, or taking severe blows to the head. He's tried to run, tried to hide, and put up a good fight. He's reached the point at which he has no choice but to temporarily surrender to his abductors in order to avoid severe bodily harm or worse.

The key word is *temporarily*. A Violent Nomad's surrender is merely a momentary play for survival.

096 Set Up Proper Posture for Escape

Get big. That's the central motto of any escape plan, and it applies at the moment of restraint.

Defeating hand restraints comes down to a matter of wrist and palm placement. Keeping the thumbs together, spread palms apart (see diagram)—this will flex the wrist muscles, broadening the diameter of the wrists. Joining the palms at thumb level will create the illusion of closed palms while leaving a sizable gap at the back of the wrists.

Frequently used as restraint devices in kidnapping and torture scenarios, chairs provide a foundation against which to brace a victim's limbs—but also a structure against which to buck and strain. At the moment of restraint, take deep breaths to increase the width of the chest, arch the lower back, straighten arms and knees as much as possible, and move feet to the outside of the chair legs. Shrinking back down to size once captors have left the room will create gaps in the restraints.

If restrained with rope or chain, attempt to discreetly create slack in the restraints by retaining a length of rope or chain in one hand (see diagram).

No. 096: Set Up Proper Posture for Escape

CONOP: Present proper postures to promote escape.

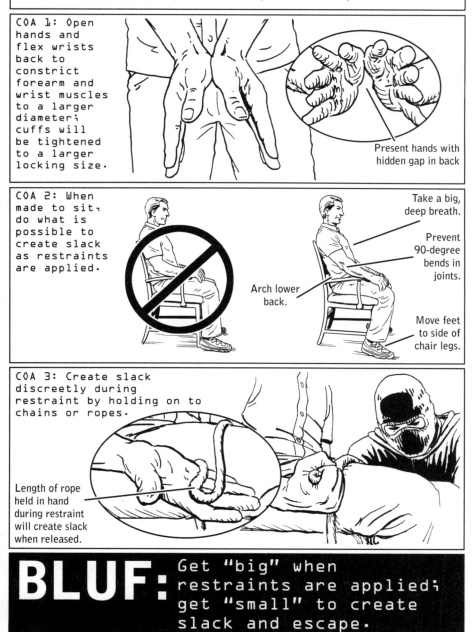

COA 1: Open hands and flex wrists back to constrict forearm and wrist muscles to a larger diameter; cuffs will be tightened to a larger locking size.

Present hands with hidden gap in back

COA 2: When made to sit, do what is possible to create slack as restraints are applied.

Take a big, deep breath.

Prevent 90-degree bends in joints.

Arch lower back.

Move feet to side of chair legs.

COA 3: Create slack discreetly during restraint by holding on to chains or ropes.

Length of rope held in hand during restraint will create slack when released.

BLUF: Get "big" when restraints are applied; get "small" to create slack and escape.

097 Reposition Restrained Hands

It bears repeating that one of the most important components of any type of restraint defeat happens at the moment of capture—when the operative temporarily "surrenders" while setting himself up for escape as best he can. An operative should present his hands in front of him if possible. Should captors be willing to restrain him in this position, he will have less work ahead of him. (As law enforcement officials know, the most effective way to subdue detainees is to restrain them with their hands behind their backs, thus preventing them from using their hands or tampering with their restraints. This is also the restraint position most often seen in combat and hostage scenarios—but it's one operatives are well equipped to defeat.)

When being restrained, spread hands and flex wrists to increase girth and improve the chances of being able to wiggle out of the restraints (see page 232). Discreetly drive forearms down into the cuffs as they're applied so that they are placed higher up on the wrists, where the diameter is larger.

Once cuffed and left alone, visually inspect the restraints in order to determine a defeat method. To do that from a posterior restraint, move both restrained hands along waistline to one side of body and look down, or leverage any available reflective surfaces (windows or mirrors) around. View restraints and determine the best course of action *before* repositioning hands—the last thing an operative wants to do is get caught with his hands in front of him without a plan.

No. 097: Reposition Restrained Hands

CONOP: Reposition restrained hands from back to front.

COA 1: Though a posterior restraint position limits range of movement, repositioning is sometimes possible.

COA 2: Pull wrists apart as hard as you can.

COA 3: Lower hands past glutes and bend at waist.

COA 4: Lower chest to knees and drop hands behind knees.

COA 5: Step through wrists one leg at a time.

COA 6: With wrists in front, it is now possible to defeat restraints.

BLUF: It's much harder to defeat the unknown. Always reposition restraints to promote successful escape.

Equal parts magic trick, criminal ruse, and defensive operational skill, the art of restraint defeat comes down to an understanding of the mechanics of the particular restraints used. Armed with a common bobby pin (preemptively tucked in at the waistband), time, and patience, anyone can eventually defeat a pair of handcuffs, particularly if they are of an extremely common make (see diagram).

If wiggling out of the cuffs isn't feasible, there are several defeat options to try: picking, shimming, or prying the cuffs apart.

Pick the Lock: To pick a common pair of handcuffs, insert one end of the bobby pin into the lock and sweep it toward the wrist until it catches. Pull up on the bobby pin to disengage the shackle arm.

Shim the Lock: The easiest method of handcuff defeat, shimming involves feeding a bobby pin or similar instrument between its teeth and ratchet. Driving down the shim temporarily tightens the cuffs, but will eventually separate the teeth from the ratchet (similarly to the action of breaking a zipper). Once the shim has been pushed down far enough, an upward pull will yank open the lock.

Pry the Shackles Apart: If handcuffed inside a vehicle, use a seatbelt tongue to break the double bows away from the shackle arm.

No. 098: Defeat Handcuffs

CONOP: Escape handcuffs using destructive and nondestructive techniques.

COA 1: Get to know the handcuffs.

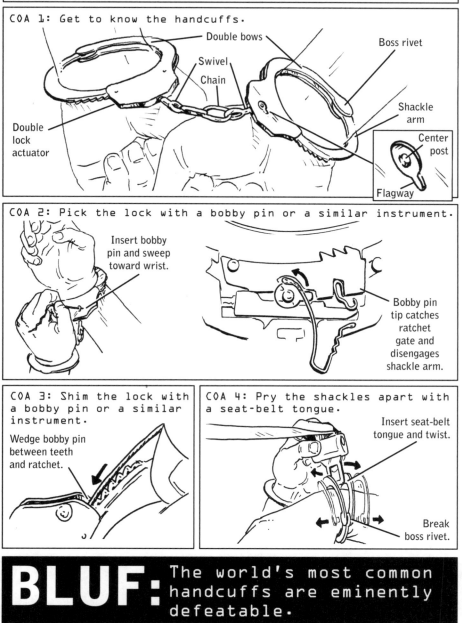

Double bows

Swivel

Chain

Boss rivet

Shackle arm

Double lock actuator

Center post

Flagway

COA 2: Pick the lock with a bobby pin or a similar instrument.

Insert bobby pin and sweep toward wrist.

Bobby pin tip catches ratchet gate and disengages shackle arm.

COA 3: Shim the lock with a bobby pin or a similar instrument.

Wedge bobby pin between teeth and ratchet.

COA 4: Pry the shackles apart with a seat-belt tongue.

Insert seat-belt tongue and twist.

Break boss rivet.

BLUF: The world's most common handcuffs are eminently defeatable.

099 Defeat Zip Ties

Efficient, streamlined, and lightweight, zip ties seem to present an optimal method of restraint for the criminals who use them. Originally designed to hold together cables and wires, once applied the ties are designed to lock permanently, typically removed by a pair of shears. Just like handcuffs, tape, and other means of restraint, however, they are eminently defeatable.

Because zip ties are made of plastic, they can be worn down by repeated friction. A cinder block or a brick or cement wall will wear them down quickly, but if a rough surface isn't available, they can easily be unlocked with a bobby pin or similar instrument.

No. 099: Defeat Zip Ties

CONOP: Use a bobby pin to defeat zip-tie restraints.

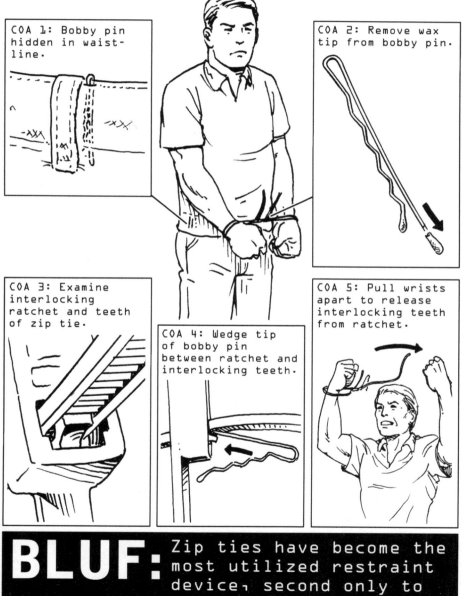

COA 1: Bobby pin hidden in waist-line.

COA 2: Remove wax tip from bobby pin.

COA 3: Examine interlocking ratchet and teeth of zip tie.

COA 4: Wedge tip of bobby pin between ratchet and interlocking teeth.

COA 5: Pull wrists apart to release interlocking teeth from ratchet.

BLUF: Zip ties have become the most utilized restraint device, second only to duct tape.

100 Defeat Duct Tape

Famous for its durability and its many applications, duct tape is the familiar stuff of school projects, banged-up car bumpers, and patchwork home-improvement jobs. More often than not, duct tape is also an abductor's restraint of first resort—readily available and inexpensive, quick and easy to apply. Once abductors have moved victims to a second location, they may upgrade to zip ties, handcuffs, or nylon cord; time-consuming to secure, particularly if they involve knots, such restraints are frequently reserved for the period following the initial abduction, when abductors have more time to tie the victim down—which makes the beginning phases of an abduction so crucial.

Defeating duct tape or packing tape may seem like an impossibility, especially when it's tightly wrapped in multiple layers. But through a shrewd use of the body, victims can break through their bonds.

Duct tape and other types of cloth-backed adhesive tape may tear more easily than shipping tape, which can harden into an undefeatable mass of hard plastic when bunched together. The key with all types of tape is to move quickly and seamlessly, using the momentum of a snapping action rather than muscle power to shear the tape apart. Whether an operative defeats ankle restraints by squatting down abruptly or snaps out of wrist restraints by knocking his arms violently into his chest, performing the action in one sudden movement will shear the tape rather than crumpling it up into a solid and undefeatable mass.

No. 100: Defeat Duct Tape

CONOP: Use body weight to shear duct tape restraints.

COA 1: Assume a standing position. Turn feet outward into a V.

COA 2: Squat down fast, driving butt to heels. Tape will shear apart, freeing ankles.

COA 3: Reposition hands from back to front. (See #097.)

COA 4: Extend bound hands forward at shoulder height, then drive elbows past rib cage. Tape will shear apart, freeing wrists.

COA 5: Escape out back doors of kidnappers' vehicle at first stop.

BLUF: Duct tape is the most commonly used restraint upon initial abduction.

The Final BLUF

The bottom line underlying each and every skill in this book is that in a world full of unexpected, ever-changing threats, an unseen army of trained civilians is a powerful weapon. When crisis strikes, it takes only a basic level of knowledge to distinguish a victim from a survivor—or from the levelheaded leader who shepherds a panicked group of would-be victims to safety.

In other words, the true purpose of this book is not to make you more dangerous, but to make you significantly safer.

A civilian with a working knowledge of the skills described in this book is a civilian who knows how to think like a predator—which will put him one step ahead of attackers and help to prevent him from becoming prey. But beyond any one particular skill, it is the Violent Nomad mindset, defined by a spirit of improvisation and an alertness to threats of all kinds, that distinguishes victims from survivors.

In order to protect the integrity of its missions, the world of special ops must by nature remain shadowy and clandestine. Nothing in this book betrays classified tactical information that could be used by enemy forces to subvert the public good. But it does provide civilians with the ability to recognize and protect themselves from a diverse array of threats.

Danger has become an increasingly common facet of modern reality—a reality in which *deadly* may have to become the new normal.

ACKNOWLEDGMENTS

I am greatly and deeply indebted to those who helped me make this book happen.

H. K. Melton was the maven and the brains behind the initial inception of this book. His passion for all things spooky, along with his own history of successful book writing, guided me down the path to publication.

Dan Mandel is my literary agent, a man who could sell ice to polar bears and throwing stars to a ninja, and an all-around great guy who kept me out of trouble.

Savannah is my little ghostwriter, or perhaps more appropriately the writer, of this book. She spent hundreds of hours talking long-distance on the phone with me, pulling from my memory everything she could to put down on these pages. Without Savannah, and her tremendous patience, skill, and diligence, this book would have never been possible.

Ted Slampyak, who was the storyboard illustrator for the hit series *Breaking Bad*, was the illustrator for this book. His creative skills are second to none, and his partnership brought this book to a level it could never have achieved without him. He is a true professional and a master of his craft.

Matthew Benjamin is my badass, wisecracking, chain-smacking editor. If not for his leadership, patience, and vast experience, this book may have never come to life.

The publication reviewers at the Pentagon, who ferried the book through a complicated review process via a number of agencies, represent a valuable system that I believe all current and former military writers should embrace. I am grateful for their time and their efforts on my behalf.

GLOSSARY

Existing at the crossroads of military operations and intelligence, Violent Nomads occupy a world filled with acronyms and codes. Below are a few of the terms that appear throughout this book.

area of operation: The region or country in which the operative will execute his mission.

BLUF: Bottom Line Up Front.

COA: courses of action.

CONOP: Concept of Operation.

diversionary device: A device that creates an explosion or visual impairment in order to divert enemy forces and allow the operative to infiltrate or escape a target area.

EDC Kit: Every Day Carry kit, the Nomad's portable system of life support and self-defense.

helo casting: Using a helicopter jump to infiltrate an area of operation.

improvised weapons: Weapons made of available materials.

pace counting: The practice of counting steps as a navigational aid in undifferentiated territory.

PIT: The Precision Immobilization Technique, a potentially lethal technique used to disable a dangerous target vehicle.

room hide: A temporary darkroom that allows an operative to perform surveillance unobserved.

Tails: An anonymous operating system that saves no information to the cloud or to the user's hard drive.

TEDD: Time, Environment, Distance, and Demeanor, the acronym used by operatives to confirm countersurveillance and tracking.

Tor: An anonymity network that prevents third parties from tracking an Internet user's location.

RESOURCES AND REFERENCES

Escape/Security

- 100deadlyskills.com.
- Escape the Wolf, www.escapethewolf.com: The author's corporate security and crisis solutions firm.
- *Emergency: This Book Will Save Your Life* by Neil Strauss
- *Surviving a Disaster: Evacuation Strategies and Emergency Kits for Staying Alive* by Tony Nester
- *When All Hell Breaks Loose: Stuff You Need to Survive When Disaster Strikes* by Cody Lundin
- *Build the Perfect Survival Kit* by John D. McCann
- *SAS Survival Handbook: How to Survive in the Wild, in Any Climate, on Land or at Sea* by John Lofty Wiseman
- Wired Magazine's Danger Room, http://www.wired.com/dangerroom/: Covers security-related tech developments.
- Door Devil, http://www.doordevil.com/: Sells doorway reinforcement kits that can actually prevent home invasions.

Lock Picking

- *Visual Guide to Lock Picking*, 3rd ed., by Mark McCloud
- *How to Open Locks with Improvised Tools: Practical, Non-Destructive Ways of Getting Back into Just About Everything When You Lose Your Keys* by Hans Conkel
- *The Complete Guide to Lock Picking* by Eddie The Wire

Military

- *My Share of the Task: A Memoir* by General Stanley McChrystal
- *Lone Survivor: The Eyewitness Account of Operation Redwing and the Lost Heroes of SEAL Team 10* by Marcus Luttrell

- *Ghost Wars: The Secret History of the CIA, Afghanistan, and Bin Laden, from the Soviet Invasion to September 10, 2001* by Steven Coll
- *The Complete Guide to Navy SEAL Fitness*, 3rd ed., by Stewart Smith
- *Get Selected for Special Forces* by Major Joseph J. Martin with Master Sergeant Rex Dodson
- Sofrep (the Special Operations Forces Situations Report), http://sofrep.com/: Provides breaking news and opinion on all matters related to the special operations forces of the United States military.

Mindset

- *On Combat: The Psychology and Physiology of Deadly Conflict in War and in Peace* by Dave Grossman with Loren W. Christensen
- *On Killing: The Psychological Cost of Learning to Kill in War and Society* by Dave Grossman
- *Sharpening the Warrior's Edge: The Psychology & Science of Training* by Bruce K. Siddle
- *Gates of Fire: An Epic Novel of the Battle of Thermopylae* by Steven Pressfield
- *Atlas Shrugged* by Ayn Rand
- Gym Jones, https://www.gymjones.com/: The website of this hardcore training gym features online training packages.

Mountaineering/Climbing

- *Kiss or Kill: Confessions of a Serial Climber* by Mark Twight
- *Extreme Alpinism: Climbing Light, Fast and High* by Mark Twight
- *The Complete Guide to Climbing and Mountaineering* by Pete Hill
- Urban Climbing, http://urban-climbing.com/: Find resources, tips, and videos on rock climbing and urban structural climbing.

Navigation/Tracking

- *Ranger Handbook* by Ranger Training Brigade, US Pentagon

- *U.S. Army Map Reading and Land Navigation Handbook* by Department of the Army
- *The SAS Tracking & Navigation Handbook* by Neil Wilson

Prep/Survival

- Benchmade, http://www.benchmade.com/: Sells top-of-the-line survival knives for outdoor enthusiasts and well-prepared citizens.
- County Comm, http://www.countycomm.com/: Sells overstocks of tactical and outdoor gear manufactured for governmental agencies.
- Huckberry, https://www.huckberry.com: High-end, stylish gear for urban adventurers.
- Imminent Threat Solutions, http://www.itstactical.com/: Sells military-grade gear ranging from trauma and survival kits to lock-picking and escape tools.
- MOTUS, http://motusworld.com/: Articles and resources for civilians ready to take their survival skills to the next level.
- Shomer-Tec, http://www.shomer-tec.com: Sells the surveillance and security equipment used by police officers and members of the military.

Spycraft

- *Spycraft: The Secret History of the CIA's Spytechs, from Communism to Al-Qaeda* by Robert Wallace and H. Keith Melton
- *The Official CIA Manual of Trickery and Deception* by H. Keith Melton and Robert Wallace
- Spy Coins, http://www.spy-coins.com/: Sells hollow coins and dead-drop devices for camouflaging microchips and sensitive documents.
- Survival Resources, http://survivalresources.com: Sells a wide variety of emergency-preparedness and survival gear and supplies.

Miscellaneous

- Tactical Distributors, http://www.tacticaldistributors.com/: Provides high-end tactical apparel and gear.

• Trikos International, http://trikos.com/: Provides of top-of-the-line personal protection canines, trained by the same methodology as the dogs that serve alongside Navy SEALs.

• The U.S. State Department's International Travel Guidelines, http://travel.state.gov/content/passports/english/country.html: Source for up-to-date security alerts and country-specific safety advisories for international travelers.

• Aircraft Owners and Pilots Association, http://flighttraining.aopa.org/learntofly/: Find piloting courses near you.

• Wingsuit Flying, http://www.wingsuitfly.com/: Learn more about wingsuit flying and find out where to get trained.

INDEX

Note: Page numbers in *italics* refer to illustrations.

About the Author

Clint Emerson, retired Navy SEAL, spent twenty years conducting special ops all over the world while attached to SEAL Team Three, the National Security Agency (NSA), and the elite SEAL Team Six. Utilizing an array of practical skills he developed to protect himself while at home and abroad, he created Violent Nomad—a personal non-kinetic capture/kill program cataloging the skills necessary to confront any predator or crisis.